Advance Praise for *Life After College*

College is easy: you get a schedule of classes and a four-year plan. Life is hard: you have to make the plan yourself. Thankfully, Jenny's book helps you make the plan, with plenty of time for both career and life itself. Jenny's great book lives up to its hefty promise—read it to get what you really want. Don't wait! "

—Chris Guillebeau, Author of *The Art of Non-Conformity*

"Jenny Blake is an overwhelmingly positive voice for the Millennial generation. Here is someone who is working her way up the ladder at one of the most prestigious companies in the world while pursuing her dream. Read this book, become Jenny's friend, and be privy to all the life skills and knowledge she has learned along the way...in Twitter-sized bites!"

—Alexandra Levit, Author of *New Job, New You: A Guide to Reinventing Yourself in a Bright New Career*

"I wish someone had given me this book twenty years ago! The wisdom and maturity behind the tips and insights in *Life After College* are simply mind-boggling coming from a twenty-something author. Jenny Blake has written a guide to life that would enlighten and equip anyone, not just college students. What a gift this book will be to anyone who is lucky enough to read it."

—Dr. Susan Biali, M.D. Wellness expert, coach, international speaker and author of *Live A Life You Love: 7 Steps to a Healthier, Happier, More Passionate You*

"Jenny was once my coaching client, and now her book is coaching ME. Yes, even experienced coaches can benefit from the back-to-basics self-examination that *Life After College* requires of its readers. The book is chockablock with tips, exercises, anecdotes and ideas that can help anyone create an independent, happy, fulfilling life."

—Ruth Ann Harnisch, President of The Harnisch Foundation and Founder of Thrillionaires.org

"*Life After College* is less a book than a compass.
It's also an interactive pep talk, a plan of attack
and a treasure trove of razor-sharp advice."

—Phil Villarreal, Author of *Secrets of a Stingy Scoundrel*

"This is your real life – not a practice life. It's important
to stop for a moment to think about what really matters to you,
what lights you up, what you truly want in life – and then to
design a roadmap to that future. Jenny's book is that roadmap.
She helps you explore your unique genius, gives you fast-acting
strategies and innovative exercises and shows you how to make
your personal and professional dreams a reality. Most people
spend more time planning their vacations than planning their
lives. Miracles will happen when you follow the inspiring
and practical advice Jenny offers. Give it as a gift to
everyone you know who wants to get the most out of life."

—Barbara Fittipaldi, CEO of Center for New Futures

"Jenny Blake's *Life After College* should be called
The Rest of Your Life After College. It's the smart, useful get-up-
and-go guide we all need to not only live big, but to live better."

—Kevin Smokler, co-founder of BookTour.com

"A book that solves all your life's problems
and gives you a big wet kiss afterwards? AWESOME!"

—Neil Pasricha, Author of *The Book of Awesome*

Life After College

The Complete Guide
to Getting What You Want

Jenny Blake

RUNNING PRESS
PHILADELPHIA · LONDON

Edited by Jennifer Kasius
Cover and Interior design by Amanda Richmond

Running Press Book Publishers
2300 Chestnut Street
Philadelphia, PA 19103-4371

Visit us on the web!
www.runningpress.com

To my family—
thank you for always encouraging me to dream big,
and for helping me believe that I am capable of
anything and everything I set my mind to.

Introduction

THERE IS NO MANUAL FOR THE REAL WORLD. IN high school and college we have teachers, guidance counselors, and course requirements. But the minute we graduate it seems we are immediately expected to understand where to go, what to do, and how to get wherever we're going next—even when we have no clue where "next" is.

For the first time in many of our lives, we feel paralyzed without a defined road map—or without any clue how to create one.

This book represents the road map I pieced together along my own journey. It is a collection of my personal experiences and tips, helpful exercises and resources, as well as quotes and advice from dozens of college graduates. It is designed to help you focus on the BIG picture of your life—your hopes, dreams, and highest aspirations. It is a jumping-off point to help you start creating the life you *really* want, and will encourage you to think outside of the box as you also learn practical tools and systems to navigate through your life after college.

ABOUT MY LIFE AFTER COLLEGE

My life after college started early—one quarter into my junior year at UCLA—when I got the opportunity of a lifetime. I took a leave of absence from school to help start an online survey research company with my political science professor and mentor, along with four other college professors. I was the youngest employee (by at least 15 years) with very little work experience, save for a few internships I had in college.

I had tremendous responsibilities at the start-up—from office manager to webmaster to marketing assistant—and l loved the confidence I got from working hard and learning so much every day. But there were also many times I felt isolated, lonely, and lost. While I was struggling to understand health insurance, my 401(k), and how to be a good employee, my friends were still partying and taking finals. I got pangs of jealousy when I heard about how much fun they were having, and questioned whether I had made the right decision (even though I knew deep down that I had).

So I read, I researched, and I set goals for myself. I became a student of personal finance, time management, organization, productivity, business, leadership, personal growth, goal-setting, health, and happiness. I read more than 150 development-related books and took courses in all of the above.

During my second year at the start-up, I returned to UCLA for one last quarter to finish school and graduate with my class in the Spring of 2005. At that point, I felt compelled to share the many resources and tips I had accumulated with others who might be as lost as I was, so I started a website (LifeAfterCollege.org) that I turned into a blog two years later.

A shining success story, right? Except that I was about to be blindsided by my very own quarter-life crisis.

Motivated by achievement— a blessing and a curse.

I have been motivated by achievement my entire life. And for the most part, it has worked very well for me. I started working full-time at the start-up company when I was 20 years old. I finished my degree from UCLA in three years with a double major and college honors.

By the time I turned 25, I had moved up the ladder at Google, completed training to be a life coach, become a manager, and tackled some of my biggest personal life goals, including running a marathon and buying a house, all while building and growing side projects like my blog and this book. And if this seems like a ridiculous list of achievements that only the foolhardy would attempt in this short period of time, you would be right. I hit—no, slammed into—a wall ... hard.

The quarter-life crisis knocked me off my turbospeed treadmill right on cue. As soon as I turned 25, I realized I was utterly exhausted. I didn't know how to maintain the same cycle of achievement, and I became incredibly sad and tired. I knew I couldn't maintain that frenzied pace for the rest of my life, but when I thought about stepping off the fast-track, I panicked. It absolutely terrified me because achievement was all I had ever known.

Awareness: planting seeds for my "ah-ha" moment.

At first I felt spoiled and absurd for feeling so unhappy, so I tried to ignore the fact that something was wrong. But pretty soon, red flags started popping up. I became an emotional wreck. I was tired and stressed. Much to my humiliation, I cried more times than I would like to admit. At work. In meetings. Each time became the new lowest moment in my career.

I knew that something needed to change after the fifth, sixth, and seventh red flag smacked me in the face. They say that what we resist persists—in this case, my body and mind continued sounding alarms until I finally listened and took steps to figure out what I truly wanted, and who I really was underneath the shiny veneer of achievement.

From a spark to a brush fire.

In 2007 I received a coaching session that changed my life. My coach asked me what I felt I was born to do, and I stuttered and stumbled through my reply. No one had ever asked me that before, but I knew the answer was that I wanted to help other young people who were lost. I wanted to help people live happy, balanced lives through practical tips and tools.

After attending my first coach training class, I turned that spark of inspiration, that clarity of my purpose, into a brush fire. I took coaching classes on my free weekends. I coached clients at night and in the early morning. I worked on projects related to coaching and development at work. I did not ask for permission to help people. I just did. And by exercising my passion, my skills grew naturally. They had room to breathe.

Finally, after countless nights spent stumbling through and exploring my life after college, I finally found my way to my dream job as a career development program manager at Google. It felt like the job was created just for me.

You are not alone in this journey.

I hope that no matter what position you are in or how many years it has been since you graduated, you will realize you are not alone out there. Change is constant, and only one thing is certain: life after college is a series of ups and downs, full of personal exploration and opportunities for growth.

Beyond the everyday aspects of adjusting to life on your own, starting a career, figuring out how to manage your money and maintaining your relationships, life after college is about realizing that you are in the driver's seat, and that you have full responsibility for your life from here on out. My hope is that this book will help you feel empowered and inspired to create the life you really want. I know you can do it, and I'll be right here to help in every way that I can.

ABOUT THIS BOOK

This book is not a narrative; it is a compilation of tips, quotes, and exercises trimmed to the essence, divided into chapters for every major life area, including: Life: Your Big Picture, Work, Money, Home, Organization, Friends & Family, Dating & Relationships, Health, Fun & Relaxation, and Personal Growth.

This book will help you create a plan; however, it is not meant to be an all-inclusive how-to guide.

I trust that you know how to use Google and that you are creative, intelligent, and resourceful. If you want specific details about apartment hunting, setting up your 401(k), or filing taxes, this book may not be for you. (I list a number of books at the end of each chapter for this purpose.)

You do not need to read the chapters in chronological order. Skip to sections that interest you, or flip to a random page every day for thought-starters, exercises, and ideas.

Please don't feel like you have to agree with every point or listen to every piece of advice—take what is helpful to you and throw out the rest. Experiment with ideas that you are curious about, take time to do the exercises (which is by far the best way to get your money's worth from this book), and feel free to correct me where you think I'm wrong!

ABOUT THE FORMAT

The information within each section is labeled to make navigating easier. Here is a legend for the types of information you'll find:

Jenny's Tips
Best practices for life after college.

Advice from College Graduates
Interviews conducted with people of all ages.

Coaching Exercises
Questions to get you thinking. Grab a pen or notebook to get the most out of these.

Deep Dives
An in-depth look at selected key topics.

Notable Quotes
Inspirational quotes from public figures.

Two Cents from Twitter
Crowd-sourced wisdom from college graduates in 140 characters or less.

Recommended Reading
Suggested books for each topic.

WRITE IN THIS BOOK.

It does not need to be handled with care. This is *your* book, ready for *your* thoughts, notes, and highlights.

1. Life: Your Big Picture

"When you get to a fork in the road, take it."
—**Yogi Berra**

BEFORE JUMPING INTO AREAS SUCH AS WORK, money, and relationships, let's take a look at the big picture of your life. Clarifying your values and goals will give you an anchor for everything you do—the compass that will help you make big decisions and find your footing when you feel unsatisfied, unfulfilled, or lost.

This chapter is about figuring out who you are, what makes you happy, and what you want for yourself. It is also about making smart decisions while taking risks; planning for the future without worrying too much about it. Finally, life is about figuring out where you fit within your broader community and leveraging your unique vision to make the world a better place.

This chapter covers:

- **Setting the "big picture" vision for your entire life**
- **Identifying your core values**
- **Brainstorming short- and long-term goals**

MY LIFE MOTTO: ONE DAY AT A TIME

*"Finish each day and be done with it. You have done what
you could; some blunders and absurdities have crept in; forget them
as soon as you can. Tomorrow is a new day; you shall begin it serenely
and with too high a spirit to be encumbered with your old nonsense."*
—Ralph Waldo Emerson

Do you want to know how great things happen? Life achievements and big scary dreams? Buying a house, living a healthy lifestyle, making it to your 60th wedding anniversary (like my grandparents), or sticking to your New Year's resolutions?

I'll tell you how. One day at a time. Let me say it again: ONE. DAY. AT. A. TIME. Sure, tomorrow is a new year, but today is a new day. Make the most of it. Take a baby step toward a goal. Give a new habit one more chance to stick. Climb one step higher up the mountain even if you are afraid of heights.

Life gets too overwhelming for me when I think about committing to something like good health, a relationship, or a house for the rest of my life. I don't know about you, but I find thoughts like that paralyzing; an open invitation for my saboteur to swoop in and show me all the ways I'll screw it up. So stop scaring yourself out of big things. You don't have to do great things all at once, for the rest of eternity. You just have to give it your best shot on any given day. And that day is today.

*"Renew thyself completely each day;
do it again, and again, and forever again."*
—Chinese inscription cited by Henry David Thoreau in *Walden*

Whether it's a new job, a big dream, or some other scary endeavor that leaves you feeling vulnerable, uncertain, or insecure—the only way you will succeed is by trusting your gut and taking baby steps. If something scares you, that just means the opportunity is big enough. And that's a great thing.

Stress is caused by regrets about the past or worries about the future. Focus on today, and trust that just for today you can honor yourself and what you really want in this life. And if you stumble? Get back up the next day and keep going. ONE. DAY. AT. A. TIME.

Just do me one favor: please remember to laugh and love yourself along the way.

JENNY'S TIPS

Spend some time reflecting on life's big questions:

- What is your life purpose? What is your unique gift to this planet? Tough questions, but once you start to figure these out, the smaller details of your life will fall into place.

- You can start to think about your life purpose in terms of what impact you want to have on other people. If you could wave a magic wand to change them in some way, how would you want them to feel? What are some of your unique gifts to facilitate that change?

For example, I believe my life purpose is to inspire others to live their best lives; to help people focus on the big picture of their lives through simple, practical exercises and tips.

- Set time aside to think about who you want to become in the next year. What do you want to change about yourself? What strengths do you want to develop? What do you believe in? What do you want your life to stand for? What do you want to be remembered by? (*There are some exercises at the end of this chapter that will help you brainstorm answers to these questions.*)

Find out what success means to YOU.

- There are two types of success: internal and external. Allow yourself to define success on your own terms—what makes you feel great. Don't wait for the external world to validate or define what success is for you.

- Try to keep your focus inward and don't compare yourself to others. You are exactly where you should be. As the saying goes, "Comparison is a losing game."

- The popular saying by Judy Garland also holds true: "Be a first rate version of yourself, not a second rate version of someone else."

Explore your personal values; use them as a compass.

- Spend some time reflecting on your values (see the values exercise later in this chapter for a head start). Values are the core operating principles by which you live your life. Your values are usually not something you choose; they reflect who you already are and what makes you feel most fulfilled.

- Notice areas where you feel stuck, conflicted, or unhappy. It is usually a sure sign that one (or more) of your values are at risk or are being stepped on.

Set specific goals and write them down.

- Less is more; it will allow you to focus on what is most important. Choose 2 or 3 major goals to focus on at any given time and tackle those first. Once you achieve them, you can always set new ones.

- Allow yourself to dream big. When you get inspired by a new idea, don't let yourself get bogged down in the "tyranny of the hows." Focus on building out the "what" of your vision before getting into the details.

- When someone tells you "no" about something that you really want, use it as an opportunity to prove to yourself (and that person) how much it actually means to you. "No" is often an opportunity to make a stronger case for "yes" or to ask in a different way.

• Motivation will inevitably dip during the pursuit of any big goal. Make a point not to get discouraged, and refocus on your vision of the best possible outcome—the reason you set the goal in the first place. Celebrate your dips as part of reaching an important milestone in the pursuit of your goal.

• Be aware that sharing your dreams with others will not always yield an enthusiastic response. You might hear things like "Are you sure?" "Is it practical?" or "That won't work." Don't let others' limited views of your possibilities discourage you. It is your unique vision or dream, and it is perfectly fine if they can't see it yet.

Be proactive about your own happiness and do your best to enjoy the journey.

• You own your life; you are responsible for it. If you aren't happy, don't just complain—focus on what you are going to do about it.

• Don't delay being happy until the future. What can you do to be happy today? Right now?

• Make a point every day to be patient, forgiving, grateful, and compassionate.

• Joy is always there if you look for it. Notice and emphasize positive feelings when they arise—stop for a moment and give those moments your full enthusiasm and awareness.

See problems and challenges as opportunities. Know that lows just mean bigger and better things are on the horizon.

• Life is what you make of it—be proactive. Be curious about the world and take every experience as a learning opportunity.

- "Problems" are actually gifts we are given to help us learn, evolve, adapt, and grow. Without challenges there would be no triumphs; without valleys there would be no peaks. Take a moment to celebrate and embrace the challenges you are facing in your life at the moment.

- Sometimes we expect life to be easy, and we get upset when it becomes hard. Life is not meant to be easy. There will always be cycles of ups and downs; life is about enjoying and appreciating the ups while learning and growing from the downs.

- Everything happens for a reason. Live your life without spending too much time questioning why things have happened to you. Look instead for how that experience might help you in the future.

- When you are ready to explode, cry, scream, yell, or bang your head against the wall, remember to BREATHE. Close your eyes and take three deep breaths. While it can be hard to remember to do this in the moment, you will be amazed at how much it helps.

- There is a saying that "what you resist persists." Sometimes giving yourself permission to feel hard and/or painful feelings allows you to work through them more quickly.

- Try approaching tough situations with the mantra "there is nothing I can't handle, even this." If that saying doesn't work for you, make up your own.

- In awareness you have a choice. Instead of mindlessly moving through life, become aware of your behavior in the moment—notice and make a conscious choice about whether to continue destructive thoughts or behavior. When it comes to limitations we create for ourselves, being aware is the first step to getting out of our own way.

Trust yourself. You know more than you think you do.

- Listen to your gut and trust your intuition. Sometimes your gut knows things your brain hasn't figured out yet.

- Make big decisions using your gut. Just because 10, 1,000, or 1 million people believe something doesn't make it true, or right for you. Learn to question assumptions and reach your own conclusions about your life.

- Trusting your gut is like building a muscle. You may have to take a few risks based on gut instinct and blind faith; then as you watch those risks and decisions pay off you will start learning to trust yourself even more in the future.

- Get clear and be specific about what you *really* want and great opportunities will be infinitely more likely to happen.

Have fun!

- Don't forget your sense of humor! Laugh, smile, and try to have fun no matter what you are doing.

- Make sure you celebrate your successes. Many people have a hard time celebrating their accomplishments. Before you move on to striving for the next big thing, take time to truly appreciate and honor how far you've come. You've earned it, and you deserve to celebrate.

- Expand your joy—stretch it out. When we are blessed with happy moments, it is a great gift to focus on soaking them up and enjoying every possible second that we can.

ADVICE FROM
COLLEGE GRADUATES

Laugh. A lot. Keep the faith, no matter how tough it gets. I look at life like a stock market curve—no matter how low it dips, it always rebounds. Don't rush. This life IS short, so enjoy each present moment of your life. Be loyal and true to yourself and those you hold most dear.
—Tara C., California State University, Sacramento

The "real world" does not open its arms to you and provide you whatever you want after graduating. It actually does take hard work and persistence to create your ideal life. After graduating, the possibilities are infinite, but they are a lot harder to obtain and you don't always end up where you thought you would be. That's also what is so exciting.
—Kristi R., St. Edwards University

Don't get so overwhelmed about your choices that you become paralyzed. Just take a step forward in any direction and try something out, even if you're scared or unsure about the outcome. That's what this age is all about; there are no mistakes, just learning experiences.
—Nerissa G., University of California, Santa Barbara

Don't worry so much about whether you're on the "right path" at this moment. Great opportunities present themselves at the most unexpected moments, in surprisingly unexpected ways. What's most important is being open and being flexible.
—LVL, Arizona State University

Find your own path! Most of us leave college full of knowledge about everything but ourselves, and full of ideas about what we should be doing from everyone but ourselves. It is impossible to find a path that fits you until you know who you are and what you want independently of what others think you should be doing. Be honest with yourself about the external pressure you feel to fit into someone else's vision of what your life should be, and let go of anything that doesn't feel like it is coming from within you.
—Adrian Klaphaak, USC

Life: Your Big Picture 21

EXERCISE:
UNCOVER YOUR VALUES

A value is a belief, a mission, or a philosophy that is meaningful to you. Whether consciously aware of them or not, every individual has a guiding set of personal values. Values are not something you choose or want in the future; they represent who you *already* are and the core principles that guide your actions. It is likely you experience strong feelings of tension or unhappiness when you are not living according to your core values; conversely, you feel most fulfilled and deeply satisfied when you *are* living according to those values.

1. Below is a list of common personal values. Read through the entire list first, then **circle the 20 values that resonate most** (feel free to write your own if you can't find what you're looking for).

Common personal values:

Accomplishment	Competence
Accountability	Competition
Accuracy	Control
Adventure	Cooperation
Authenticity	Creativity
Autonomy	Decisiveness
Beauty	Delight of being, joy
Belonging	Democracy
Calm (inner peace)	Discipline
Challenge	Discovery
Change	Duty
Cleanliness	Ease of use
Collaboration	Efficiency
Commitment	Equality
Communication	Excellence
Community	Excitement

Exploring	Openness
Fairness	Passion
Faith	Patriotism
Family	Peace, nonviolence
Flexibility	Perfection
Freedom	Persistence
Friendship	Personal growth
Fun	Physical vitality
Generosity	Pleasure
Global view	Positive attitude
Good will	Power
Gratitude	Practicality
Growth	Preservation
Happiness	Privacy
Hard work	Problem-solving
Harmony	Progress
Health	Quality of work
Helping	Quiet
Honesty	Regularity
Honor	Resourcefulness
Humor	Respect for others
Independence	Responsiveness
Innovation	Results-oriented
Inspiration	Risks, taking
Integrity	Safety
Intimacy	Satisfying others
Justice	Security
Kindness	Self-reliance
Knowledge	Service (to others, society)
Leadership	Sharing
Love	Simplicity
Loyalty	Skill
Meaning	Speed
Merit	Spirituality
Modesty	Stability
Money, wealth	Status

Strength	Tradition
Structure	Tranquility
Success, achievement	Truth
Systemization	Uninhibited
Teamwork	Unity
Tenacity	Variety
Timeliness	Warmth
Tolerance	Well-being

2. Now narrow that list to ten. Write them below.

_____   _____

_____   _____

_____   _____

_____   _____

_____   _____

3. Choose your top five values and rank them from most important to least important. This may be harder than it sounds; you may want to reflect on this and come back to it tomorrow or later in the week. _(This exercise took me about two weeks of ordering and reordering my list; you might also put the top 10 on Post-Its on a wall of your house, then rearrange them until you are happy with the order.)_

My top five values (subject to change):

_____

_____

_____

_____

_____

4. Value Strings—The words we use for our values mean different things to different people. Value strings can help create a more complete and personalized picture for each of the values you have identified. For each of your top values, add words that capture what you mean—like a game of word association.

The words or phrases used in your value string do not have to be values themselves—they can be subjective or intuitive things that capture a feeling or idea, like "grand canyon" or "on top of the world."

Here is a sample value string:

Personal Growth / learning / growing / challenging myself / living big! / expanding my awareness / teaching / mentoring / inspiring others

My value strings:

1. Value 1: _____ / _____ / _____

   _____ / _____ / _____

2. Value 2: _____ / _____ / _____

   _____ / _____ / _____

3. Value 3: _____ / _____ / _____

   _____ / _____ / _____

4. Value 4: _____ / _____ / _____

_____ / _____ / _____

5. Value 5: _____ / _____ / _____

_____ / _____ / _____

A side note (and my personal values list):

The words you use to represent your values don't all have to be terms that you find in this section. Feel free to get creative and make something up! Here is a list of my personal values—you can see that some are quite unique (but to me they convey each sentiment perfectly):

FREEDOM—Freedom to be myself, freedom to be honest, and freedom to live an independent life. Freedom to be able to support myself financially and emotionally (I never want to stay in a relationship or job because I'm afraid to leave). Look within to achieve balance and serenity; do not rely on others for my happiness.

SERVICE—Use my talents to serve others; to inspire, motivate, teach, and uplift people in service of living their best lives. Dedicate my life to helping others reach their full potential; to feel empowered, happy, confident, and creative.

PHYSICAL VITALITY—Express myself fully by doing what I love. Commit to healthy sleep, fitness, and nutrition habits in order to maintain physical vitality for long-term health and happiness. Honor my body and treat it like a well-oiled machine; love and accept myself despite any perceived flaws.

GRATITUDE—Take time every day to appreciate and give thanks for my health, my family, my friends, my job, my ability to give back to others, and all the small things that make me feel incredibly fortunate. Regularly express my gratitude to others.

GROWTH—Enjoy the process of learning from people and situations in my life. Learn from my failures and my successes. Find new ways to challenge and stretch myself through reading, further education, and new experiences.

CUPCAKES!—Honor my playful, fun side. Celebrate often! Indulge, be happy, relax, and look for ways to expand pleasure and joy in my life.

CLEAN-BURNING FIRE—Contribute positive energy to the world. Bring optimism, good cheer, and a smile to a room or a conversation whenever I can. Be conscious of my impact on others; don't leave a dark cloud of smoke behind—focus on being a passionate, happy, shining light.

RIDE THE WILD TIGER—Live big! Take risks! Leap! Go big or go home. Do things that make me uncomfortable—that challenge what I think is possible. Ride the wild tiger—there is no saddle; there are no reins to hold on to. Just enjoy and adjust to the crazy ups, downs, and surprises that life throws my way.

EXERCISE:
YOUR LIFE REPORT CARD

Rate your current level of satisfaction (on a scale of 1–10) in each of the following areas of your life (these areas are also the chapters of this book). Consider how you are feeling right now, and know that your ratings on this report card will constantly change. Doing periodic check-ins can help you figure out where you are doing well, where you feel disconnected or stuck, and in what areas you are looking for more balance and satisfaction.

_____ Work

_____ Money

_____ Home

_____ Organization

_____ Friends

_____ Family

_____ Dating & Relationships

_____ Health

_____ Fun & Relaxation

_____ Personal Growth

EXERCISE:
DREAM LIFE BRAINSTORM

Now that you have rated how you currently feel about each area of your life, it is time to articulate what you really want.

For this exercise, describe what a "ten" in each area would look and feel like. What do you want to have, do, or be one year from now?

Work

_____

_____

_____

_____

_____

Money

_____

_____

_____

_____

Home

_____

_____

_____

_____

Organization

_____

_____

_____

_____

_____

Friends

_____

_____

_____

_____

_____

Family

_____

_____

_____

_____

_____

Dating & relationships

_____

_____

_____

_____

_____

Health

_____

_____

_____

_____

_____

Fun & relaxation

_____

_____

_____

_____

_____

Personal growth

_____

_____

_____

_____

_____

Other

_____

_____

_____

_____

_____

EXERCISE:
GOAL BRAINSTORM

The final step after articulating your vision for each area of your life is to set goals based on specific things you would like to do, have, feel, and learn in the next year.

Writing down your goals is a powerful step toward actually making them happen. On the next page there is a table for brainstorming 6-month, 1-year, and 3-year goals. Give yourself 15 minutes to write down as many things as you can in each of the squares (refer back to the previous exercise for a head start). When you think you are done, push yourself to add a few more in each category (those might be some of your most creative ideas).

Note: It's fine to leave some of the squares blank. For example, you may not have goals related to skills and education for every single block of time. Likewise, sometimes the "be/feel" column is consistent no matter what the time frame. If that is the case, just fill in the top square.

Goal brainstorm

	Things You Want to DO	Things You Want to HAVE	How you want to BE/FEEL	Skill or Education
6 MONTHS				
1 YEAR				
3 YEARS				

DEEP DIVE:
BIG, SCARY, HAIRY GOALS

Big, Scary, Hairy Goals. You know what I am talking about—those goals of yours that seem so big and scary that you can barely bring yourself to admit that they exist. BSHGs require their own special set of observations:

Writing them down can be hard because you may be afraid to fail; there is a lot at stake, and you may not be sure you can actually achieve the goal.

Saying them out loud is often the scariest part. Saying them out loud to another person (who is awake and listening) is even scarier, but it makes the goal start to feel REAL (and maybe even possible).

When someone first tells you a goal of theirs, especially a BSHG, congratulate them! Say nothing about practical considerations or what might stop them—so often those remarks are about our own baggage or perceived limitations, not theirs. Likewise, don't let others' limited beliefs hold you back. It is *your* unique goal, not theirs—so it makes sense that not everyone will be able to see the possibilities right away.

The bigger and more important the goal (in a life-fulfilling kind of way), the louder and more insistent the "inner critic" becomes. Inner critics (also referred to as gremlins or saboteurs) are those voices that try to bring you down or protect the status quo with phrases like "you are not experienced/smart/unique enough to reach that goal" or "you can't do that—who do you think you are?" We all have inner critics. Learn to notice the difference between these voices and what you *know* to be true. (There is more on this in the Personal Growth chapter.)

If you stop referring to your goals as scary, it starts to take the scariness away. "Scary" just means the opportunity is big enough. Our language creates our reality. Be proud and excited when you share your big goals with others! Don't shrink away from them.

Setting BSHGs and working toward them feels REALLY good. That does NOT mean it feels easy or effortless. But it does feel really great to stretch and expand beyond what you originally thought was possible for yourself. It feels even better to learn, grow, and inspire others in the process. Finally, it feels great to fail and know that you can pick yourself back up. So get out there! Don't be afraid to get dirty.

EXERCISE: BSHG CAPTURE

What would you do if you knew you could not fail? Pretend you can freeze time and work on something without anyone knowing about it or judging your success (at least until you're ready).

_____

_____

_____

What would you be most proud to achieve in your lifetime?

_____

_____

_____

What are some of the inner-critic messages that get in the way of you setting or pursuing your biggest goals?

_____

_____

_____

What advice would you give yourself in response to your inner critic?

_____

_____

_____

DEEP DIVE: STICKY GOALS

Setting goals is a relatively straightforward process. Pick something you want to do or have and write a statement that is specific, measurable, action-oriented, realistic, and time-bound (the SMART formula). However, *sticking* to the goals you have set is an entirely different story.

Some goals are slippery—they never really seem graspable, and before you know it you have forgotten all about them. Really meaningful goals are sticky—they take on a life of their own, and you cannot help but work on them consistently and tirelessly until you reach them.

The following strategies helped me stick to my goal of running a marathon in 2008—a goal that once seemed utterly impossible quickly became rewarding and enjoyable.

Get inspired.

I had been tiptoeing around the idea of running a marathon for almost a year before I finally committed. I started to realize that every time someone mentioned they were training for or had finished a marathon, I was jealous. Then, one day after admitting on my blog that I "was still too scared to train for a marathon" a reader (complete stranger) wrote back with a link to a video on YouTube called "Running My First Marathon." I was so inspired after watching the video that I committed to myself right then and there.

Getting (and staying) inspired, whether by videos, friends, family or a cause that is important to you, is an incredibly important part of sticking to a goal—it is what recharges your battery when you are ready to quit.

Make a symbolic "I'm serious" purchase that will help you in your pursuit of the goal.

As soon as I committed to running the marathon, I splurged on a pair of custom Nike+ running shoes that were wirelessly connected to my iPod. I ordered them in UCLA colors (go Bruins!) and had my motto, *Live Big!*, sewn into the back. Those were my lucky shoes for the rest of training (and every event I've done since). Lacing them up for training runs made me feel like a serious runner, and I wasn't about to back out on my new shoes; I was determined to take them all the way to race day!

Set up regular accountability.

As soon as I committed to my goal, I called my dad, a marathon veteran, and let him know. I also wrote ten questions on a piece of paper, and asked if he would help keep me accountable by reviewing them with me every Sunday. Questions like, "Did you do your long run?" "What did you learn from running this week?" and "Are you having fun?" helped keep me on track and focused not just on the goal, but on the process too. Plus, I knew I couldn't get away with completely quitting—what would I tell my dad on Sunday?

Visualize success.

I can't stress enough the importance of visualizing success—seeing yourself from the perspective of already achieving your goal. It creates a positive reality to work toward, and cements what success will be like. I designed a SELF magazine cover (featuring me) and taped it to my bathroom mirror to visually represent my goal. I also wrote a "feature" article as if I were being interviewed about the diet and exercise habits that led to my success, and visualized how great I felt as a result.

When my morale dipped during training, I would make a point to re-connect with my original vision and picture myself crossing the finish line at the actual marathon, surrounded by friends and family, and how elated and proud I would feel.

Consider the alternative—
not sticking to your goal.

The alternative to sticking to my goal was giving up. When I thought about giving up, I thought about how that would make me feel. I would feel deflated, discouraged, and disappointed. As challenging as it was to get motivated sometimes, I knew it would feel far worse to let myself down.

Avoid the All or Nothing trap.

Maybe you have experienced this before: giving up on a goal after just one slight misstep. I call this the All or Nothing trap—it's the feeling that if I can't do something 100%, I shouldn't do it at all. Or if I veer off course, I might as well stop and let everything fall apart rather than make an adjustment and get right back on track.

Don't make a big deal out of getting off track. Just pick yourself up and keep going right where you left off. In fact, "getting off track" often provides a much-needed break.

Don't forget about gratitude.

Rather than complain about how miserable I was during my runs, I made an effort to focus on everything I was thankful for. When running got tough, my inner dialogue would start something like this: "I'm tired. My feet hurt. I'm hot and thirsty. I have so far to go."

At that point I would stop and purposefully shift gears to "I'm thankful that I am able to run at all. That I am healthy and strong. That my body is willing to put up with me throughout this crazy training process. That I get 5 hours outdoors to think and be alone. I am thankful that I get to enjoy nature—the blue sky, the birds, the water, and the people-watching. I am thankful for the huge boost in self-esteem I feel after I finish a long run. I am thankful for my supportive friends and family, who encourage me every step of the way."

Take your goal one hour, one day, one week at a time.

At many points during my early weeks of training, I got completely overwhelmed at the thought of running 21 miles on my own, let alone a full marathon. At that point I felt like 8 miles was my maximum, and 21 seemed absolutely impossible. I had to constantly remind myself not to worry about the future weeks—just the next Saturday's long run. I told myself I will have plenty of opportunities to worry about those longer runs later, so why start now?

Don't let yourself get scared away by the magnitude of your goal. What makes it sticky is breaking it down in to smaller steps that seem more possible, steps that build to create confidence and stickiness. Once you have started working on your goal (and told friends, family, and co-workers), you are truly invested and it is a lot harder to give up and walk away.

Little by little, week by week, I built on the previous weeks' accomplishments and was able to achieve just a little bit more, until the very moment when I actually crossed the finish line during the marathon itself. It was one of the proudest moments of my life.

EXERCISE: STICKY GOAL STRATEGY BRAINSTORM

What are some methods that have helped you commit to your goals in the past?

_____

_____

_____

_____

What are some new tactics that might help you stick to your goals in the future?

1. _____

2. _____

3. _____

4. _____

5. _____

What is important to you about sticking to your goals and seeing them to completion?

_____

_____

_____

_____

_____

EXERCISE: MAKE ENVY WORK FOR YOU

Envy may be one of the seven deadly sins, but it can also be a powerful tool to help figure out who you want to be, what you want to have, and how to go after both.

In this exercise, you'll put your envy to work for you. It might sound strange to highlight jealousy or envy when it is something so often associated with being negative. But you can put that jealousy to constructive use by honing in on things you want in your future.

Instructions

In the left-hand column write the names of people you envy or admire (whether it is for something they have, something they do, or qualities they possess). These can be people you know, acquaintances, or public figures. In the right-hand column, list all the reasons you have chosen that person.

Try not to censor yourself—write down everything that comes to mind, whether it is something frivolous (like a fancy car) or more substantial (like generosity). Continue adding to this list throughout the next two weeks, then circle common themes and key areas you want to work on.

When I completed this exercise, I had almost all of my friends, family, and mentors listed on my sheet of paper. I found that for almost every person in my life, there is something they are doing or that they have that I admire and want to strive for. And that is what makes them great people to have around!

The other good news is that you already have a list of people you can speak with to learn more about how each of them got where they are. And don't forget that you have qualities and aspects of your life that others admire too!

Name	Qualities and Achievements You Admire

TWO CENTS FROM TWITTER

Finish this sentence: When I graduated from college I wish I had known . . .

@tracytilly There IS life (happiness) after college. It's called networking and happy hour!

@LMSandelin College taught me more about myself than my chosen career path . . . and to be honest, I value that education more.

@dmbosstone I wish I knew I was supposed to be taking risks and getting lost—not trying to settle down and find a job.

@pandroff You won't have as much free time as you think. Don't overcommit & be sure to schedule both social time and me-time.

@kelseyonthego There is always more to figure out; we all stumble before we soar—no rush.

@Rlibby01 Getting out of credit card debt takes about 10x as long as getting in.

@sjhalestorm That decisions aren't final.

@sameve The most difficult experiences often teach you the most. If you can't find the silver lining, try something new.

NOTABLE QUOTES

The best way to predict the future is to create it.
—Alan Kay

Be who you are and say what you feel because those who mind don't matter and those who matter don't mind.
—Dr. Seuss

You miss 100 percent of the shots you never take.
—Wayne Gretzky

Try to learn to breathe deeply, really to taste food when you eat, and when you sleep really to sleep. Try as much as possible to be wholly alive with all your might, and when you laugh, laugh like hell. And when you get angry, get good and angry. Try to be alive. You will be dead soon enough.
—William Saroyan

Neither stress nor happiness is contained in things, events, or situations. Things are just things, events are merely events, situations are only situations. It's up to you to supply your reaction to them. You get to choose.
—Chris Prentiss

As long as you are going to be thinking anyway, think big.
—Donald Trump

If you limit your choices only to what seems possible or reasonable, you disconnect yourself from what you truly want, and all that is left is a compromise.
—Robert Fritz

The foolish man seeks happiness in the distance,
the wise man grows it under his feet.
—James Oppenheim

You may be disappointed if you fail, but you
are doomed if you don't try.
—Beverly Sills

Most people have attained their greatest success
just one step beyond their greatest failure.
—Napoleon Hill

Success is the ability to go from one failure to
another with no loss of enthusiasm.
—Sir Winston Churchill

I've found that luck is quite predictable. If you want
more luck, take more chances. Be more active. Show up more often.
—Brian Tracy

Live as if you were to die tomorrow.
Learn as if you were to live forever.
—Mahatma Gandhi

Anyone who stops learning is old, whether at twenty or eighty.
—Henry Ford

You do not fail in life, you only produce results, and you have the right
to learn and grow from any results that you produce.
—Wayne Dyer

Experience is what you get when you didn't get what you wanted.
And experience is often the most valuable thing you have to offer.
—Randy Pausch

To be independent of public opinion is the first
formal condition of achieving anything great.
—Georg Hegel

Be patient toward all that is unresolved in your heart
and try to love the questions themselves.
—Rainer Maria Rilke

Keep on beginning and failing. Each time you fail,
start all over again, and you will grow stronger until you
have accomplished a purpose—not the one you began
with perhaps, but one you'll be glad to remember.
—Anne Sullivan

Let life happen to you. Believe me: life is in the right, always.
—Rainer Maria Rilke

Everything you do right now ripples outward and
affects everyone. Your posture can shine your heart or
transmit anxiety. Your breath can radiate love or muddy the
room in depression. Your glance can awaken joy. Your words
can inspire freedom. Your every act can open hearts and minds.
—David Deida

The secret of getting ahead is getting started.
The secret to getting started is breaking your complex overwhelming
tasks into small manageable tasks and then starting on the first one.
—Mark Twain

The time to repair the roof is when the sun is shining.
—John F. Kennedy

Take the first step in faith. You don't have
to see the whole staircase, just take the first step.
—Martin Luther King Jr.

RECOMMENDED READING

Finding Your Own North Star: Claiming the Life You Were Meant to Live
Martha Beck

How to Be, Do, or Have Anything: A Practical Guide to Creative Empowerment
Laurence Boldt

Zen And the Art of Happiness
Chris Prentiss

Maximum Achievement: Strategies and Skills That Will Unlock Your Hidden Powers to Succeed
Brian Tracy

The Last Lecture
Randy Pausch and Jeffrey Zaslow

Influencer: The Power to Change Anything
Kerry Patterson, Joseph Grenny, David Maxfield, Ron McMillan, and Al Switzler

The Dip: A Little Book That Teaches You When to Quit (and When to Stick)
Seth Godin

Feel the Fear and Do It Anyway
Susan Jeffers

The Joy Diet: 10 Daily Practices for a Happier Life
Martha Beck

Life After School Explained: The Definitive Reference Guide
Cap & Compass

The Art of Non-Conformity: Set Your Own Rules,
Live the Life You Want and Change the World
Chris Guillebeau

Gradspot.com's Guide to Life After College
Chris Schonberger

20 Something Manifesto: Quarter-Lifers Speak Out About
Who They Are, What They Want, and How to Get it
Christine Hassler

2. Work

"Formal education will make you a living;
self-education will make you a fortune."
—**Jim Rohn**

W E SPEND THE MAJORITY OF OUR WAKING HOURS at work. Producing work that engages our mind and our creative capabilities can be the greatest feeling in the world. Toiling at the entry level filing papers and stocking office supplies can feel mind numbing—but only if you let it. They call it "work" for a reason—it isn't always fun and games. You can learn from almost every situation and person you encounter—consider it part of your ongoing post-college education.

We all work for different reasons. At a minimum, our jobs help pay the bills. At best, our jobs also allow us to grow, learn, contribute, collaborate, and feel fulfilled. Despite how much of your identity may be wonderfully shaped by the work that you do—don't forget this very important fact: you are not your job. You are a creative, interesting, independent individual with your own ideas, aspirations, interests, and insights.

This chapter is about:

- Navigating the workplace with professionalism
- Surviving life at the entry level
- Building a strong reputation
- Laying a foundation for your long-term career
- Discovering what you are passionate about
- Defining what effective work/life balance means to you

MY WORK MOTTO: DON'T WAIT

Don't wait for other people to make you happy.

Don't wait for your manager to ask you what you need.

Don't wait for your job to become fulfilling on its own.

Don't wait for your work/life balance to magically settle where you want it.

Do get crystal clear on what you want.

Figure out what makes you happy through trial and error.

Focus on your strengths and grow them.

Pay attention to when you feel most "in the zone" and do more of it.

Collect as many lessons and experiences as you can—good and bad.

Keep what works and magnify it; grow it into something bigger.

Not 100% satisfied with your full-time job?

Talk to your manager and start a conversation.

Start something on the side. *Today.*

Stop delaying your happiness until tomorrow.

Above all, commit to being a leader in your own life.

Commit to taking charge.

Commit to you making yourself happy—in life and work.; no one else is going to do it for you.

JENNY'S TIPS

Be a proactive and engaged team player. Make yourself indispensable.

- Anticipate the skills you will need 6 months or 1 year from now. Be proactive about seeking learning opportunities to position yourself for a new role or promotion in the future.

- If something is bothering you, fix it. If you can't fix it, get over it.

- Anticipate and get started on work that needs to be done before others ask you to do it.

- Add value. Every day, every meeting, every task.

- Be firm with your commitments. If you say you're going to do something, do it. If you can't, let the person know in advance and renegotiate.

- Ditch the phrase, "I'll try." You will either do something or you won't. Be clear with the person asking what you will deliver and by when. If there is just no way you can help, be up front about it and let them know. If you're not sure, tell them you need some time to think about the request.

- Be able to tie your work to the bottom line. How are you contributing to the goals and success of your team and of the company?

- Take a pen and notebook to meetings. If you bring your laptop, keep it closed unless you are taking notes; it is often too distracting otherwise.

- Be cheerful! Say hello in the mornings; spend time making the rounds. People will appreciate your positive attitude.

- Be a team player. Help others even when you are busy, without expecting anything in return.

- Don't complain if you don't have a solution or idea for how to fix something. Be known as a problem solver.

- Regardless of your level, make a point to be a leader on your team and in the company.

• Focus on doing the best you possibly can with any task or project. Attention to detail and focusing on quality might take time, but they are skills that will pay dividends in the long run.

Treat every day as a valuable learning opportunity.

• You are not above any task or job—especially at the entry level. Use small jobs to show your skill—those are the easiest to go the extra mile on anyway.

• Observe and learn from everyone in the office. How can your skills complement theirs? How can you make their job easier and vice versa?

• Humble yourself. Don't get defensive; do not take constructive feedback personally. Take criticism as advice to help you grow stronger—it usually is.

• Write down words, phrases, or abbreviations you don't know that come up during meetings or conversations. If you feel silly asking about what they mean, you can look them up later.

• Focus on learning from your mistakes. Bad day? Reflect on what you will do differently next time.

• You are allowed to make most mistakes once. Admit when you have made a mistake, focus on the lesson, and move on.

• Take advantage of company training opportunities. If you are not learning and growing, you will quickly become obsolete.

• Be open and honest with your manager. Invite feedback. Ask what skills they think you'll need to be successful in the future.

• Be observant; learn from the success and failure of others.

Stay focused and organized; prioritize your work and don't procrastinate.

- Jump into tasks immediately—the longer you put things off, the more stress you create for yourself. Make a list of your three most important tasks at the start of each day and work on those first.

- Keep instant messaging at work to a minimum—it can be distracting and disruptive if it's not work-related.

- Go for a walk in the afternoon if you are feeling tired or stressed. The fresh air and exercise will clear your mind and make you more productive for the rest of the day.

- If you are overwhelmed by a task or project, break it down into smaller tasks until it becomes clear what to do next.

- Be ready to hand a project over to someone at any time. Keep your work organized and easy to follow in case someone else needs to pick up where you left off.

Help tame the e-mail beast: keep e-mails short, sweet, and work-related.

- Assume someone is reading your company e-mails. Keep all personal e-mails in a separate account.

- Don't be "that guy (or girl)" who accidentally replies all with an embarrassing or rude comment. Double-check the "to" field before hitting send.

- Keep e-mails short and to the point. Be clear with requests and deadlines. Use descriptive subject lines and highlight any specific action items or requests within the e-mail.

- Consider using your e-mail inbox as a to-do list. File e-mails you are finished with after responding or taking action.

- As many productivity gurus recommend, if you can respond to an e-mail in less than two minutes, do it. Don't let small tasks pile up.

- Plan your day before you get sucked into answering e-mails. Work on your biggest priorities before jumping in to reactive tasks.

Perception creates reality; think carefully about the image you project at work.

- You will develop a reputation at work whether you like it or not. Remember that everything you do, wear and say WILL be judged. Do everything you can to act with integrity and make a good impression on your co-workers.

- Invest in your wardrobe. A few key pieces are better than many cheap ones if they help you feel confident and comfortable.

- As the old adage goes, "Dress for the job you want, not the job you have."

- With some exceptions, your co-workers are not your friends. Keep drinking at company parties to a minimum, and keep relationships professional. If you have to vent, at least do it with friends outside of work. Even better, go directly to the source and try to clear things up.

- Speak up in meetings, but do your best to back up your opinions with examples and facts (where appropriate).

Relationships matter: get to know others, say thank you, and treat people with respect.

- Do not underestimate the power of informal conversations and relationship-building. You never know when you will need to work with someone you meet on a project or have to ask him or her for a favor.

- Keep a personal document or journal where you record observations about people in positions you would like to hold one day. What do they do well? What would you do differently? What makes them successful? What skills do they have that you need to develop?

- Make eye contact. It shows confidence and builds trust.

- No matter how nice people are at your company, at the end of the day it is still a business. They don't owe you anything, and unless you provide value every single day, they are not obligated to keep you around.

- Be direct with your co-workers; if you have an issue, talk to them about it. Don't let resentment or frustration stew—it will only make things worse.

- Acknowledge people when they have helped you or done something to impress you. Always say thank you. Remember how good it feels to be recognized for your work and that compliments are free!

- Remember that your boss or manager is a person too. Treat him or her with respect and kindness. Give him or her the benefit of the doubt.

- Be on time. It shows that you respect others' time.

Keep it classy (and legal!).

- On racist jokes, sexual comments, and otherwise unethical activities: if you are not sure, do not do it. At best, you risk getting scolded and damage your reputation. At worst, you risk get fired and possibly sued.

- If someone tells you something in confidentiality, keep it that way. Nothing spreads faster than office gossip.

- Treat everyone with respect. Realize that your opinion is one perspective, one version of the truth. It is typically not the only version.

- Hooking up with and/or dating your co-workers can be risky business, especially if you work in the same building or general area. Although many people meet their significant others at work, be extra cautious about crossing the line if the other person is on your same team or you work at a small company.

- Order a set of personal business cards that you can hand out at conferences and events if you are connecting with people for things unrelated to your job. (I get MiniCards from Moo.com.)

Job hunting? A few résumé tips:

- When describing tasks that you did in previous roles, focus on IMPACT: what were the results of the work that you did? Use numbers and metrics wherever possible.

- In addition to listing general job activities for each position, provide examples of one or two projects you worked on, including your specific contributions and the impact of your work on the company.

- Include a "summary of qualifications" at the top of your résumé that gives recruiters a snapshot of who you are. What are your biggest strengths and unique talents? How has all of your experience blended together to create a compelling and useful set of skills? How can you benefit the team or company?

- Don't sacrifice quality (design or content) just to get your résumé to fit on one page; however, it should still be concise and easy to read. Choose the highlights and most meaningful experiences.

- Include an interests section; it will give recruiters and interviewers some insight into your personality, and will provide fun talking points so that they can get to know you better. Most employers aren't looking for drones—they are looking for well-rounded, interesting individuals who will be productive AND fun to work with.

- Take a few online assessments (such as Myers-Briggs or Strengths-Finder 2.0) to learn more about your unique strengths and personality type.

- These tests can also help you identify potential career paths and give you language to better articulate your strengths to future employers. Collect your results and store them in a "master file" that you can refer to as you put together your résumé or prepare for interviews.

Remember, you are not your job.

- There is really no such thing as perfect, fixed work/life balance. Your work is 80% of your life. Make the most of it, and do what you can to enjoy it. That said, make sure to create a rich and fulfilling life outside of work too.

- Know that you will have bad days and good days. Learn from the bad and keep them in perspective—how much will it matter to you in 2 weeks or 2 months?

DEEP DIVE: A NEW TAKE ON WORK/LIFE BALANCE

I've got a bone to pick with the term "work/life balance." What does it mean to balance our work and our life if our work is such a big part of our lives? Are we supposed to check our lives at the door, and only start living them before we get to the office and after we leave?

Given that we spend so much time at work, the more important question is: how can we integrate our work and our lives so that we flow seamlessly from one area to the next, maintaining an overall state of aliveness and energy?

We can start by not forcing balance, but rather adjusting and readjusting in a state of flow as we notice ups and downs in our energy or stress levels. These pointers are from a workshop I did with my good friend and fellow life coach, Jenny Ferry.

Myths about work/life balance:

- That "life" starts as soon as we leave the office.
- That there is an ethereal scale hanging in the sky, and the sides will perfectly balance.
- That once you figure things out, life will stay balanced (when in reality there is no "there" where you have achieved total balance forever).
- That we have total control over how big the various pieces of our life "pie" are at any given time.
- That being unbalanced is always a bad thing (sometimes you need things to be unbalanced so you can really go after what you want).
- That you will finish your to-do list and it will be done forever. There will always be things to do —don't let the list control your life.

New perspectives on the work/life challenge:

- It is all about flow—don't beat yourself up when things get out of balance, just notice and adjust.
- Be okay with where you are in the moment; try not to carry guilt about the things you didn't get done.
- Acknowledge work as a huge part of our lives, not something to run away from; it brings confidence, sense of accomplishment, and social interaction with others.
- Try taking a moment-to-moment perspective. Ask yourself, "What do I need right now?"
- Let go of the notion that "I'm supposed to have it all YESTERDAY" (the great job, the great house, the great relationship, the great bank account balance).
- Realize that we cook up so much of what we "should" be doing in our own mind—for most of us there is not a real person cracking a whip telling us what to do, saying "get everything on your to-do list done!"

We put a lot of pressure on ourselves, and sometimes we create more stress than we need to. Relax a little bit and release some of the need for control.

- Take a bird's-eye view and refocus on the bigger picture agenda for your life. How much will what you are worrying about matter in 5 months or 5 years?

- Try to create balance within each day. Exercise, call a friend, go to work, do something restful.

Tips for managing work/life balance:

- UNPLUG! With Twitter, Facebook, blogs and e-mail, life can easily seem to center around the chaos coming from your computer and cell phone. Balance may mean prying yourself away from your electronics to go be outside or do something fun.

- Exercise can be a great way to unwind and transition to a different state of mind.

- Make a point to relax, schedule time with friends, and have fun.

- Try journaling—it may help you become more aware of where you are satisfied and where you want more.

- Kick yourself out of the "I'll start tomorrow" mentality about things that are making you unhappy. Start now!

- Awareness. When you are not happy, try to get clear on why and what might move the situation forward. Become an observer of your thoughts and behavior.

- When you are stressed, pick the three most important things on your to-do list and just focus on those.

- Block out specific time each day or week to slow down and reflect.

- Make a list of what you've accomplished each day (rather than focusing on the things you didn't get done).

EXERCISE: AIM FOR
BALANCE WITHIN EACH DAY

It helps to think about balance in small bits—balance within in each day. For example, what can I do tomorrow to live according to my values? I can go to the gym, call a friend, prioritize my tasks at work, and set ten minutes aside to think about something I'm really passionate about. By aiming for balance within the day, and repeating that, I move toward balance in life without getting overwhelmed.

What does "balance within the day" look like for you?

_____

_____

_____

_____

_____

What 3 specific actions could you take to improve your life balance?

1. _____

2. _____

3. _____

DEEP DIVE: YOU DON'T ALWAYS HAVE TO PURSUE YOUR PASSION FULL-TIME

Don't get me wrong. I am all about figuring out what makes you happy, vigorously taking control of your career, and making changes so that you don't get run into the ground doing work you don't like, love, or—gasp!—aren't passionate about.

This might sound hypocritical given my general stance on doing what you love, but I want to acknowledge that there is a time and a place for pursuing your passion full-time, and it is different for everyone.

There is a lot of talk in the personal growth field about pursuing your passion and following your dreams. And I think that is fan-freaking-tastic whenever you are READY for it. Don't feel bad if you're not ready today. Don't let fear hold you back, but learn to separate fear from actually getting value out of where you are now.

And that doesn't mean throwing your passion out the window. Commit to carving out time every week to cultivate activities and start building a vocation you really love. If it's volunteering, do it! If it is writing, do that. If you can figure out how to do these things within your job description; even better! It's not a zero-sum game—you don't have to pursue your passions full-time in order to have them enrich your life.

What are some steps you could take toward discovering or pursuing your passion, even with a full-time job?

_____

_____

_____

_____

DEEP DIVE:
10 REASONS I LOVE MY CUBICLE

Even though I fantasize sometimes about traveling the world while working from anywhere, let me tell you a secret: I also love cube life. And don't feel bad if you do too. Heck, even if it's not love—you can still find a lot to appreciate about the 40-plus hour-a-week office job that often gets a bad rap.

I am sharing this list because I want to encourage those of you who may feel you've settled or are somehow stuck in the dreaded rat race just because you "work for the man" at an office job. *That said, if you're not currently doing work that suits you, where you sit won't really matter. For help thinking about next steps in your career, see the exercises at the end of this chapter.*

1. **I love working in an open, collaborative environment.** I learn so much from my co-workers; in meetings, at lunch, and passing in the hallways.

2. **It's nice to have someone to share, vent, or laugh with.** I love spinning around in my rolling chair, tapping my co-worker on the shoulder and asking for advice, input on a project, or taking a quick chat break. It keeps me sane! Personal, face-to-face connections with co-workers are priceless.

3. **I love structure.** The 9:00 to 6:00 schedule really works for me. I wake up, go to the gym, work a full day, go to yoga, have dinner, and go home. I'm fulfilled by having a routine, and don't see it as being a prisoner at all.

4. **I love meeting new people**. I live alone, so I'm glad I don't also work alone right now. Working for a company, especially a large one, is a great way to meet new people, particularly for those of us trying to make new friends and expand our social circles.

5. **Office supplies galore!** Here's another secret about me: as a kid, I loved office supplies more than candy. One of the perks of working in an office: you get free office supplies! Just about whenever you need them! It's beautiful.

6. **Boring but true: benefits, benefits, benefits.** I love that I don't have to figure out how to get health insurance, a 401(k), or a Flexible Spending Account on my own. I fill out a handy questionnaire online, and POW! Everything is taken care of.

7. **Get this: I like having a manager!** Yes, it's true. I love being a leader too, but I learn so much from people with more experience than me. I like having someone who asks questions about my work, who gives me feedback, holds me accountable, and who reflects on my strengths and development areas. I've also learned as much from bad managers as I have from good ones; both of which help me be a better worker, leader, and manager myself.

8. **Working for a company is like being in the middle of a business school case study as it is being written.** I love being an observer of how companies operate—all the way from a start-up to a big company like Google. What systems are in place across the company? What works? What doesn't? How do leaders motivate their employees? What demotivates them? I love being able to observe and learn lessons about business and leadership, all without going into $150K of debt.

9. **When the printer says "PC Load Letter" I don't have to fix it** (or beat it with a baseball bat like the guys in the movie *Office Space*). Don't get me wrong—I'm a master at fixing copier jams. I get a weird sense of satisfaction from opening EVERY SINGLE door and turning every damn handle until I fix the stupid thing. But I'm still thankful that I don't need to purchase or maintain expensive office equipment.

10. **I will love the location independent lifestyle even more when I get there.** Working in a cube—enjoying it AND getting it out of my system—will really help me enjoy and appreciate the location independent lifestyle when I finally take the plunge one day. I'll know what I'm leaving behind—the good and bad—and find ways to re-create the good when I'm on my own.

A Final Note: May we all find our own freedom in our everyday lives, cube or not.

DEEP DIVE: 10 TIPS FOR MOVING UP THE CORPORATE LADDER

1. **Don't just focus on promotion as an end in itself.** It's like losing weight: you can either focus solely on the number on the scale or on getting healthy overall. Getting healthy has many more benefits. Similarly, don't just focus on the promotion itself. Focus more on the competencies, expectations, and behavior that will lead to a promotion; you'll be better off in the long run and most likely get there faster.

2. **As Carol Bartz, CEO of Yahoo!, advises: build your career like a pyramid not a ladder.** Don't be afraid of horizontal moves. Focus on finding work that is soul-stirring (as Tim Gunn would say) and make adjustments along the way. It is much better for most people to focus on finding work that is a great fit rather than just on getting promoted. Sometimes you have to make a lateral move, but if it leads to greater happiness and productivity, it is probably worth it in the long run.

3. **Have the right conversations.** Try asking your manager the following questions: What does success in my role look like? In 3 to 6 months, what would you love to see me doing? What else should I be doing to operate at the next level?

4. **Be an observer.** Pay attention to people who have been recently promoted or who work in the level above you. What skills, experience, and attitudes do they have?

5. **Ditch the entitlement.** You may think you deserve a promotion (and you might be right) but also be aware that much of the time people think they deserve promotions earlier than their managers might think so. Be willing to compromise and navigate this through open, direct conversations. Remember that it often depends on many factors outside of your job performance alone (such as the economy and other people in the company).

6. **Networking is key.** There will often be more people involved in deciding whether to promote you than just your direct manager. Try to get experience working on projects that involve other leaders within the company.

7. **Want a promotion? Ask for more responsibility instead.** In many companies, you have to already be operating at the next level before you get promoted. Keep this in mind, and continue asking for increased responsibility (and/or additional side projects).

8. **Stand out.** Make yourself indispensable by being proactive, having a positive attitude, and being a flexible team player. Come up with ideas and solve problems before your manager asks. Do what it takes to be their right hand.

9. **Focus on impact, not just output.** As you are taking on more responsibility, focus on delivering quality work that makes an impact. Be able to show that the work you are doing is improving the company in a material way (for example: increasing sales, making processes more efficient, making programs more effective).

10. **Don't sacrifice your sanity just to work toward a promotion.** It's not worth it! You'll get angrier and angrier if the promotion doesn't come right away, but mostly because YOU are giving too much. Keep the balance and remember to have fun, even as you're trying to move up the ladder.

ADVICE FROM COLLEGE GRADUATES

Don't sell yourself short. When you go into a job interview just be confident. The funny thing about college is that it teaches you principles, but doesn't actually teach you what you will be doing at work. Every job is different and you learn 90% of it on the job. Remember that the company doesn't expect you to know how to do everything on the first day—they will teach you what you need to know.
—Vanessa M., USC

Don't stress out. When you finish school you are going to be a little lost. You are going to be responsible for work that you may not know how to accomplish right away. The trick is to remember to stay open-minded and not be afraid to seek answers from others. Ask questions and be humble, stay hungry, and be open-minded. Everything else should start falling into place.
—Boaz N., University of Colorado, Boulder

Do something you like. I fell in love with river guiding in college and have continued to do that during the summers. Don't be afraid to quit your job if you hate it. If you don't get yourself into binding financial situations (loans, credit card debt), you will always have the flexibility to try something new and follow your passions.
—Tessa S., UCLA

Expect to pay your dues at the beginning of your career, but remember that work isn't everything. Don't kill yourself working 16-hour days just to get ahead. Some managers may just think you have horrible time management skills, and even if you finish all the work, you will just be given more. And avoid working from home if possible. Once you start checking work e-mail on evenings and on weekends, it's a hard habit to break.
—Vincent Chiaro, University of California, Berkeley

DEEP DIVE: THE BENEFITS OF VOLUNTEERING

by Grace Boyle, SmallHandsBigIdeas.com

It can be easy to put volunteering on the back burner; however, there are many reasons to get out there anyway. When I volunteer I don't have to think about my job, my stresses, or my social life. Volunteering helps me focus on being selfless and allows me to work toward something that creates a better community, and ultimately a better world to live in.

Four key reasons to volunteer:

1. **Find paid employment opportunities.** I started volunteering at a nonprofit one summer while in college. I quickly found myself learning, expanding my network, and enjoying myself. After three months of volunteering and putting in extra hours, I was offered a paid managerial position and a full-time job after graduation. Volunteering can lead to full-time employment and really helps get your foot in the door.
2. **Network; build and understand your community.** When I relocated to a new city, I was slowly making friends but I didn't feel like I understood the "pulse" of my city. Volunteering surrounded me with intelligent, forward thinking, powerful people in the community. It has created a pipeline of resources and a network in my city I can always fall back on.
3. **Improve your quality of life as well as others'.** Volunteering doesn't just benefit the people you serve. According to the Home Office Citizenship Survey, 63% of 25- to 34-year-olds say volunteering helps them feel less stressed.
4. **Make a difference.** I always say it's the little things that count, even if it's just giving two hours a week of your time. One person can create change. Be that person.

To find volunteer opportunities in your area, check out:
VolunteerMatch.org, CharityGuide.org, and Serve.gov.

DEEP DIVE: IF YOU ARE NOT LEARNING, YOU ARE OBSOLETE

"Anyone who stops learning is old, whether at twenty or eighty."
—**Henry Ford**

We all know the old adage, "You learn something new every day." Well, that is not enough. Let me rephrase that—it is not enough to get ahead. If you learn something new every day, it means you are keeping up with everyone else. Especially because for many people, learning happens passively. Someone mentions a random tidbit of trivia in conversation. You hear an unfamiliar word and Google it. That is playing defense— you won't progress if you don't take a more aggressive approach and actually set a longer-term game plan for your personal learning.

Looking for job security? Learn new skills. Become an expert in an area related to your field. Create a plan for developing universal skills that will serve you well in any company, like leadership, creative thinking, and project management. Dedicate time every week to stretching your brain, just like you would any other muscle.

The most successful people (in life and work) are those who proactively pursue learning every chance they get through books, blogs, podcasts, journal articles, magazines, speeches, mentors, and life experience.

Companies must constantly evolve and innovate to stay ahead of the competition and to continue making a profit, given that the world and its technologies get more complex every day. The same applies to you; if you are not learning, you will become obsolete.

Questions to help you create a learning plan:

Just like they say "dress for the job you want, not the job you have." What's the job you really want? What skills or knowledge do you need to get there?

_____

_____

_____

_____

Learning does not have to be job-related. What really excites you? For example: art, history, creative writing, politics?

_____

_____

_____

_____

What did you learn this week? Schedule time to reflect upon what you have learned on a regular basis. (This will be much more effective if you write it down and commit to a certain amount of time for reflection, like 15 or 30 minutes per week.)

_____

_____

_____

_____

DEEP DIVE: THE POWER OF INFORMAL INTERVIEWS

When most people hear the word interview, usually cringing and slight nausea follow. Enter the *informal* interview, where the pressure of your future is not on the line. These interviews are more like conversations, and can come in handy for learning, relationship-building, decision-making, and goal-setting.

In addition to the practical benefits, informal interviews provide a great way to strengthen your relationships (old and new), and learn interesting things about other people. Your interviewees will enjoy sharing their wisdom, and you will learn new things in the process.

Experiment with informal interviews by setting up lunches, 30-minute phone calls, coffee, or any other format that works for you. For each category, come up with at least 3 people you could meet with.

New job or job role:
One of the best ways to get up to speed in a new job is to talk to other people who are already doing it and ask them for advice; for example, what they have learned in the role and what they wished they knew when they started.

Potential people to meet with:

_____

_____

_____

Big goals:
Once you have set a big goal, like learning a second language or becoming a manager at work, talk to people who have done it before you. This type of informal interview has two side benefits: a growing support net-

work, and increased accountability as you share your goal with more people.

Potential people to meet with:

_____

_____

_____

Future career options:

Meet with someone in a completely different career path and/or company than the one you are currently in. As you meet people through friends, at conferences or at coffee shops, ask about their job. If any jump out at you as particularly interesting, schedule some time to learn more about what they do and how that person got there.

Potential people to meet with:

_____

_____

_____

People you admire:

In the last chapter you made a list of people you admire. Spend more time with these people! Tell them you admire them. Ask them to be your mentors. These are some of your most important relationships because they can help remind you of what you aspire to and how you aspire to be, keeping in mind that you are unique and wonderful in your own right.

Potential people to meet with:

_____

_____

_____

Help with decision-making:

Sometimes your friends and family, as great as they are, do not have enough information to help you through a big decision, like whether or not to go to graduate school. Interview people with a variety of experiences to gather information (for example, those who did and did not go). You are not asking for advice here—you are asking about what decisions and trade-offs your interviewees made and how satisfied they are with their choices.

Potential people to meet with:

_____

_____

_____

Last but not least,
don't forget to send thank-you notes!

While e-mails are convenient, handwritten notes are a much nicer touch and leave a lasting impression.

EXERCISE: DOWN THE RABBIT HOLE— A CREATIVE CAREER EXPLORATION

Sometimes we get so bogged down in the practicalities of life—paying bills, having and maintaining a steady income, building our résumés— that we lose sight of what makes us tick. Whether you are trying to find a career path or looking to fill needs that your current job does not quite meet, this exercise can help you discover buried interests and explore uncharted territory.

Childhood dream:

When you were a child, what did you want to be when you grew up? Who did you look up to? What jobs did you pretend to have?

_____

_____

_____

_____

_____

Guilty pleasure:

What is one "guilty pleasure" job or career that you wish you could try but hesitate to tell people about because it "wouldn't be practical" or because it is so different from what you do now? (For example, mine is being an NFL cheerleader.) List jobs that are the polar opposite of your current job or projected career path. What is appealing about them?

_____

_____

_____

_____

Unlimited resources:

The classic question—if you had unlimited time and money, what would you be doing? If you won the lottery and didn't have to work another day in your life, what would you do? Where would you live? How would you spend your time? Be outrageous!

_____

_____

_____

_____

_____

Stop and read back through your answers.

What do the various jobs and answers have in common? What are the recurring themes? How do your answers form a complete (if contradictory) picture? Do any new insights materialize?

_____

_____

_____

_____

_____

DEEP DIVE: STRESS HAPPENS, WHADDAYA GONNA DO ABOUT IT?

I have studied many methods for organizing, communicating, strategizing, and time-managing, and you know what? Stress still happens. My goal is not so much to eliminate stress forever (this would surely be a futile task) but to recognize stress when it shows up and actually do something about it. The way I see it, you can either take it out on everyone around you (like a contagious flu) or recognize that you are stressed and develop some coping mechanisms.

There are many stress reduction techniques out there. Here are a few small things you can try that make a big difference:

1. **Recognize that it is there,** and that you *do* have a choice about how to respond.
2. **Stop and get perspective.** How much will this matter in 2 weeks or 2 months?
3. **Breathe.** Close your eyes and take at least 3 deep breaths in a row. Allow yourself to slow down and really feel each breath go in and out of your body.
4. **Walk.** Get some fresh air—take a 5-minute walk alone or with a friend (employ the breathing techniques here if you can).
5. **Write.** Spend 5 minutes making a list of everything that is contributing to your stress. It's okay if you don't do anything about it right away.
6. **Forgive.** Be forgiving with yourself. Don't multiply the stress by feeling bad or upset that it is there in the first place. Give yourself credit for all the positive things you are doing and remember that in the grand scheme of things, life will work itself out.

Stress happens. It happens to the best of us. It is not whether you get stressed that matters, it is what you do when it shows up.

Stress-busting techniques:

How do you typically respond to stress?

_____

_____

_____

_____

_____

How do you want to respond to stress in the future?

_____

_____

_____

_____

What are some stress-busting strategies that might work for you?

1. _____

2. _____

3. _____

4. _____

5. _____

6. _____

7. _____

8. _____

9. _____

EXERCISE: JOB INTERVIEW ONE-SHEETER—YOUR PERSONAL CLIFFSNOTES

I prepare for job interviews like I used to study for finals: by creating a "CliffsNotes" reference guide with short buzz words and answers to potential questions. You can take these notes with you to your interview (or have them handy for a phone screen), but usually just preparing the one-sheeter will help lock the talking-points into your brain.

Five key points:

The top 3 to 5 things I want the interviewer to remember about me (highlight key strengths):

1. _____

2. _____

3. _____

4. _____

5. _____

This is why I rock:

Stories/examples that show I'm a rock star and uniquely suited for this position:

1. _____

2. _____

3. _____

4. _____

5. _____

Work 77

Areas for development:

Answers to that dreaded "tell me about your weaknesses" question:

1. _____

2. _____

3. _____

4. _____

5. _____

Brilliant ideas:

Based on what I know about the company, my suggestions for improvement or future direction of the team or product:

1. _____

2. _____

3. _____

4. _____

5. _____

My overall work/team philosophy:

How I generally approach challenges and opportunities (and a few notes about what excites me):

1. _____

2. _____

3. _____

4. _____

5. _____

Questions I have:

About the role, interviewer, company, future growth opportunities, etc.:

1. _____

2. _____

3. _____

4. _____

5. _____

My short- and long-term goals:

How this role fits well in my career plans. Why do I want THIS position? What makes me a good fit?

1. _____

2. _____

3. _____

4. _____

5. _____

Specific challenges:

What are some specific challenges I've faced, and how did I overcome them?

1. _____

2. _____

3. _____

4. _____

5. _____

EXERCISE: CREATE A PROFESSIONAL DEVELOPMENT STRATEGY

Professional development is a topic I feel strongly about and one that is close to my heart as a life coach and career development program manager. My role is to help people grow and take ownership over their lives and career, and to make sure I'm setting a good example by doing the same.

So how do you set a professional development strategy? Just as companies and teams set quarterly growth targets and business development goals, this exercise will help you take a holistic look at where you are now versus where you want to be in 6 months to 1 year.

Working through the areas below will give you clarity and focus, and will help you be more proactive about setting your own career direction (instead of waiting for a manager or company to do it for you). You may want to refer back to the other exercises in this chapter to set goals that bring together all of your previous answers.

Part 1: Current inventory & future state

KNOWLEDGE

Knowledge is directly within your control. Learning more about a subject takes time, but it is generally a very straightforward process. Blogs, books, podcasts, videos, interviews, classes—the resources available to you are vast and largely free. Commit to learning and being a sponge; it will set you apart and make you an invaluable resource to any team.

Key questions: What will it take to become an expert in your role, or in one specific area of your domain? What 2 or 3 topics of focus would be most beneficial to you? What knowledge or expertise do you want to have 1 year from now?

_____

_____

_____

SKILLS

Skills are defined as "the learned capacity to carry out predetermined results often with the minimum outlay of time, energy, or both." In plain English: skills are things that you are good at; things you have picked up over time that transfer to job-related success.

Examples of general skills are time management, project management, and prioritization. You may also have specific skills related to your job or industry, such as marketing, sales, or web development. While some skills may come more naturally to you than others, you can generally improve your skills through repetition, attention, self-awareness, and feedback.

Current state: What skills do you already have?

_____   _____   _____

_____   _____   _____

_____   _____   _____

_____   _____   _____

Future (1 year from now): What new skills would take you from average (or above average) to absolute rock star?

_____   _____   _____

_____   _____   _____

TALENTS/STRENGTHS

Talents, or gifts, are skills that come naturally to you. Talents light you up, give you energy, and make you feel like you are "in the zone" when you are fully utilizing them. You may be talented at organizing information. Someone else might be talented at singing. I am talented at motivating people and simplifying complex problems. Tapping into your talents and your natural strengths will make you infinitely more successful in your role, and help you feel happier and more engaged.

There are several professional assessments that can also help you understand your talents: Myers-Briggs, StrengthsFinder 2.0, VIA Signature Strengths, and True Colors are some of my favorites.

Current state: What skills or tasks come most naturally to you? When do you feel most "in the zone"?

_____ _____

_____ _____

_____ _____

Future: What talents are you underutilizing today? How can you better use your talents in the job you have now?

_____

_____

_____

EXPERIENCE

Experience is tried and true on-the-job learning, and unfortunately, you can't manufacture it. Particularly for young employees, "lack of experience" can be an exasperating reason for not landing a job or position you want.

Even without years of experience under your belt, you can work to understand what types of experience you will need to be successful in the future.

Current state: What are your biggest "résumé highlights" to-date? What experience(s) are you most proud of?

_____

_____

_____

Future: What job-related experience are you lacking and how can you develop those skills another way? What aspects of that experience can you learn from others?

_____

_____

_____

Part 2: Set two big career development goals

Now that we've figured out the "what," we get to brainstorm some ideas for the "how." It's time to write some measurable goals and come up with a plan for how you will research and achieve these goals. I suggest the following 5 steps:

1. **Choose two key areas of development.** Make sure they are broad and aggressive; don't sell yourself short or let yourself off easy! Stretch, think big, aim for the stars. If you aim high and fall short? You're still a success! It's far better than playing small from the start, plus you will likely learn a great deal from the milestones you don't hit.

2. **Write a mini 1-year vision statement for each area**. Write as if you have already achieved success or made significant progress; for example, "Time Management: I am extremely efficient. Each morning I focus on completing my biggest task before answering e-mails. I prioritize my work on a daily and weekly basis, and make sure that 80% of my time is focused on the top 20% of my job in terms of strategic importance."

3. **Set benchmarks for yourself**. If the development areas stretch over 1 year, what do you hope to achieve 6 months from now? Brainstorm a list of resources or action steps to help you reach your benchmarks. This may include any of the following:
   • Resources (blogs, books, videos, podcasts)
   • Training/Education (classes—online or in-person, formal education)
   • People to Talk to (Mentors, others strong in this area)
   • Other (journaling, scheduling weekly time for reflection, etc.)

4. **Develop a system to track your progress.**

5. **Engage others**. Ask for feedback regularly. If you can, partner with someone who also wants to develop in one of the areas you have chosen.

AREA FOR DEVELOPMENT #1

Goal: What is your developmental goal? What would success look like? What will you do by when, and how will you know if you are successful?

_____

_____

_____

_____

Benefits: What are the benefits of this goal? What will keep you motivated when you encounter challenges?

_____

_____

_____

_____

Steps: What steps will you take? Come up with 4 key milestones that will help you reach your goal (with deadlines).

1. _____

2. _____

3. _____

4. _____

Resources: What classes, books, blogs, people, etc. will help you develop in this area?

_____

_____

_____

_____

AREA FOR DEVELOPMENT #2

Goal: What is your developmental goal? What would success look like? What will you do by when, and how will you know if you are successful?

_____

_____

_____

_____

Benefits: What are the benefits of this goal? What will keep you motivated when you encounter challenges?

_____

_____

_____

_____

Steps: What steps will you take? Come up with 4 key milestones that will help you reach your goal (with deadlines).

1. _____

2. _____

3. _____

4. _____

Resources: What classes, books, blogs, people, etc. will help you develop in this area?

_____

_____

_____

_____

Work 85

TWO CENTS FROM TWITTER

What is the best career advice anyone ever gave you?

@opheliaswebb Work for the position you want not just the position you have.

@akhilak Go above and beyond the job at hand . . . be proactive, and bring in your own ideas to make things run better and faster.

@bitty_boop Don't be afraid to speak up. How is anyone going to know your ideas if you don't say anything?

@LMSandelin Don't feel like you have to know the answers to everything . . . in truth, no one really does.

@firstgenprofess Network with a drive to find, connect, and grow with professionals engaged in compelling work that fascinates you.

@seanathompson Instead of words of advice, I watch my colleagues and emulate the best ones. You can learn so much from seeing what one DOES.

@KunbreCoach Joining a local Toastmasters or public speaking course will generate more credibility, confidence, and opportunities.

@IrishHeart416 First impression is everything. Clothes, attitude, carriage. It takes one second to make an impression but months to change it.

@amfunderburk1 When you start to apply for jobs, clean up your social media sites. Employers can and WILL look.

@dmbosstone Don't freak out if you don't get a job right away. It's not about finding the perfect job, it's about exploring.

@davidstehle Don't be too proud to accept an entry-level position. Right now, you just need to get your foot in the door.

NOTABLE QUOTES

Success isn't permanent, and failure isn't fatal.
—Mike Ditka

Whether you think you can or you think you can't—you are right.
—Henry Ford

*You can learn new things at any time in your life if you're
willing to be a beginner. If you actually learn to like being
a beginner, the whole world opens up to you.*
—Barbara Sher

Underpromise; overdeliver.
—Tom Peters

Never mistake activity for achievement.
—John Wooden

*Hard work spotlights the character of people: some turn up their
sleeves, some turn up their noses, and some don't turn up at all.*
—Sam Ewing

*Live neither in the past nor in the future, but let each day's work ab-
sorb your entire energies, and satisfy your widest ambition.*
—Sir William Osler

*I'm a great believer in luck, and
I find the harder I work the more I have of it.*
—Thomas Jefferson

When your work speaks for itself, don't interrupt.
—Henry Kaiser

Be more concerned with your character than your reputation, because your character is what you really are, while your reputation is merely what others think you are.
—John Wooden

Oh, you hate your job? Why didn't you say so? They have a support group for that. It's called EVERYBODY, and they meet at the bar.
—Drew Carey

No one lives long enough to learn everything they need to learn starting from scratch. To be successful, we absolutely, positively have to find people who have already paid the price to learn the things that we need to learn to achieve our goals.
—Brian Tracy

It's better to hang out with people better than you. Pick out associates whose behavior is better than yours and you'll drift in that direction.
—Warren Buffett

Work is either fun or drudgery. It depends on your attitude. I like fun.
—Colleen C. Barrett

It takes 20 years to build a reputation and five minutes to ruin it. If you think about that, you'll do things differently.
—Warren Buffett

It is so easy to quit, to turn back, to give in. Never do so. Try again, and again. Try harder, smarter, but try again.
—John Wooden

Three Rules of Work: Out of clutter find simplicity; from discord find harmony; in the middle of difficulty lies opportunity.
—Albert Einstein

RECOMMENDED READING

@ the Entry Level: On Survival, Success, &
Your Calling as a Young Professional
Michael Ball

They Don't Teach Corporate in College:
A Twenty-Something's Guide to the Business World
Alexandra Levit

Getting from College to Career:
90 Things to Do Before You Join the Real World
Lindsey Pollak

Do More Great Work.
Michael Bungay Stanier

What Color Is Your Parachute?
A Practical Manual for Job-Hunters and Career-Changers
Richard Nelson Bolles

60 Seconds and You're Hired!
Robin Ryan

Conscious Business: How To Build Value Through Values
Fred Kofman

How to Find the Work You Love
Laurence Boldt

Z.B.A.: Zen of Business Administration—
How Zen Practice Can Transform Your Work and Your Life
Marc Lesser

Who Moved My Cheese? An Amazing Way to
Deal with Change in Your Work and in Your Life
Spencer Johnson, M.D.

The 80/20 Principle: The Secret to Success
Achieving More with Less
Richard Koch

3. Money

"Money is only a tool. It will take you wherever you wish,
but it will not replace you as the driver."
—**Ayn Rand**

Graduation may signal the first time your parents hand over the financial reins—cell phone bill and rent included. Or you may have been on your own for much longer, and maybe even worked to pay your way through school. Many of us graduate with thousands of dollars in student loans.

Regardless of where you land after graduation, money is a vital tool for getting what you want. Like classes in college, a little studying goes a long way when it comes to learning sound financial practices. Getting the basics down is a lot more straightforward than you might think.

If you only learn 3 things from this chapter, let them be this: spend less than you earn, pay your bills on time, and start saving money immediately. The habit of saving money early and often will fund your dreams for the rest of your life.

This chapter covers:

- **Strategies for saving money and managing spending**
- **Creative ways to earn extra income**
- **Prioritizing paying off your debt**
- **Breaking bad financial habits**
- **Identifying what is important to you beyond money itself**

MY MONEY MOTTO: MONEY IS A MEANS, NOT AN END

Raise your hand if you would like more money (or just keep reading).

Keep your hand raised if you have a clear idea of what *values* money allows you to honor. If you're like most people, you probably haven't thought too much about the second statement.

Money is a means, not an end; it is not about buying stuff—it is about what that stuff can ultimately create for you. After taking care of our basic necessities, it doesn't mean very much to have or spend more money if you don't know how those actions will make your life better. At the end of the day, what value do you hope that stack of bills (or fancy new purchase) will add to your life?

For example, I scraped together every penny I had to buy a condo when I was 24 years old. It meant signing a 30-year mortgage—a big commitment for a young person, especially considering I still don't know where I will want to live in 2 years, let alone 30.

So why did I buy the condo, when for many this responsibility would feel overwhelming and burdensome? Because it honors a key value of mine: independence. Living on my own and supporting myself are very important to me, and the condo helps me build equity to support my financial future. If I valued spontaneity more, I might have made a very different decision, such as traveling the world for a year (which also sounds fantastic!).

Remember that wealth comes in many forms. Hopefully at the end of our lives, we will all be made far richer from relationships and experiences than by the dollars in our bank accounts. Money can certainly help you experience new things and achieve some of your goals, but it is not everything. Not even close.

JENNY'S TIPS

Conduct a "State of the Union" for your finances and sign up for an online money management system.

- It is critical that before you graduate (and forever after) you have a complete understanding of your financial situation. You should know how much you will owe on student loans, what your monthly payments will be, whether you have any credit card debt, and how much your bills and other expenses (like rent) will be each month.

- I also recommend signing up for a money management tool online for monitoring your accounts and tracking spending. My favorite is Mint.com because you can access it from almost anywhere (and opt-in to weekly or monthly reports), and the interface is clear and easy to use.

Develop sound saving habits from the start.

- Set up an emergency fund and a long-term savings account (I use ING Direct), with automatic direct deposits from your regular checking account. Even if you only contribute $10 per month to each, it will start you off on the right foot and help you develop strong saving habits. Once you get your first job, you will already have a system in place for saving money.

Be mindful about your money.

- Life is a classroom. We make mistakes so we can learn and grow from them, and hopefully avoid the same ones in the future. Take some time to learn from your current financial situation—what are you doing well? Where can you improve?

- While saving is important, you work hard so you can enjoy life and spend money on things that are important to you. Find a balance between saving and enjoying your hard-earned money.

- When hanging out with friends, be mindful of the varying range in salaries. If one person is making big bucks as a consultant or investment banker, and another is barely scraping by as a teacher, don't eat at the most expensive restaurant in town.

- Do your research before making major purchases. Read reviews, check prices online and in stores, and find out about service plans, warrantees, and return policies in advance.

- There is no shame in moving back in with your parents after graduation, especially if it will help you save money, and better still if it helps you develop good saving and spending habits.

- If you do move home after graduation, review with your parents whether they expect you to pay rent and other expenses like groceries. If not, save at least 50% of your salary as a benchmark (or save the approximate rent you'd be paying in your area plus 15%).

- Budgets can be overwhelming. Focus on four key monthly numbers: total income, money allocated to saving, "must-have"expenses (bills, rent, food), and "nice to have"expenses (drinks with friends, nice dinners, new clothes). Anything left over is yours to spend! *(See the exercise at the end of this chapter for help setting up a very simple budget.)*

Save, save, save. Start by setting up an emergency fund and a retirement savings account.

- If your company offers a 401(k) plan, JOIN. If they match, do everything you can to max out their contribution. It's free money!

- You don't achieve financial success overnight, which may make saving seem hard or impossible. Start small and go in increments—save 5% of your paycheck to start, then bump it up to 10% in 6 months, and maybe even 15% 6 months after that.

- Everyone should have an emergency fund for rainy days, unexpected car repairs or unexpected anything. A good rule of thumb is 3 months living expenses. If that's not doable, shoot for at least 1 month.

- Be disciplined about your emergency fund. Don't dip into it for small or frivolous things—it is a slippery slope that will defeat the purpose of having a back-up account in the first place.

Leverage the power of compound interest.

- Compound interest is an incredibly powerful financial concept. The earlier you start saving, the more your interest your money will earn, which over the long-term will snowball far beyond your original investment. The longer you wait to start saving, the harder each penny has to work.

- For example, if you save $1,000, and it earns 10% interest per year, you now have $1,100. Without saving another dime, when you multiply $1,100 by 10% the next year, you end up with $1,210 (you've earned $210 through compound interest). In five years, you'll have $610 of extra money without ever having added any money beyond your original investment. (For an online compound interest calculator, visit Young-Money.com.)

Automate your financial processes to make life easier.

- Direct deposit is a must—before you ever spend a dime, make sure part of every paycheck is directly deposited into a retirement account AND an emergency fund.

- If your bank has Bill Pay, use it—the bank will send checks to payees regularly or when you tell it to. This works great for paying rent because you don't have to remember to write a check every month or worry about being late—the bank will write and send the check for you.

- For bills that are the same every month, you may want to opt-in to their auto-pay option if that's an option. I do this with my utility bill, but have a limit set. If the bill is higher than $20 (my monthly average is about $15), the system sends me an e-mail instead of paying the bill.

- For bills that vary more from month-to-month or that you want to keep a close eye on (like cell phone bills), you may not want to automate payment. See if you can at least set up an e-mail alert to notify you when the next bill is due. That way you can check to make sure everything looks correct (and dispute anything if necessary) before paying.

- Use monthly e-mail notifications as a to-do list for your bills. File the e-mail once the bill is paid.

When things get financially rough, your first instinct may be to ignore your credit card bill and bank accounts, and hope things get better. They won't. Hiding from your financial problems only makes a bad situation worse.

- Use credit wisely and pay your credit card in full every month. Period.

- If you have a shopping or spending weakness, set up another bank account for that category of spending. Have money direct-deposited into that account (for clothes or trips with friends) and only spend what you earn in that account.

- Small expenses add up quickly—lunch here, coffee there. Be aware of how much you are spending on small purchases each month and adjust if necessary.

- Check your credit reports from all three major agencies once a year (I use AnnualCreditReport.com). If anything looks suspicious or wrong, make sure to call the credit agencies and investigate.

- Some purchases are worth spending extra money on; things you will use frequently (a cell phone or camera) or more expensive models that will perform substantially better than their lower-priced counterparts (like computers).

- To keep spending under control, make a list of big purchases you want to make in the next 6 months to 1 year. Prioritize the list in order of importance, then buy the items in that order. Adjust if you change your mind.

- If you are a big weekend spender, give yourself a budget in cash (rather than using your credit card)—it will make you more aware of how much you are spending throughout the weekend.

- Credit cards, while often abused, can make tracking your spending much easier than tracking cash. If you can learn to spend within your means, using your credit card often is not a bad thing. (I use Mint.com online and downloaded the Mint app to my phone. The spending distribution pie charts are amazing!)

Don't let pressure to buy extravagant gifts break your bank account.

- Extravagant gift-giving can escalate quickly—someone gives you a gift that would be out of your price range, so you feel compelled to match the cost when you reciprocate. This can go on for years, where one or both of you is stretched beyond your comfort zone. Set a limit for gifts and stick to it; thoughtful and creative gifts are more meaningful anyway.

- Holiday gift-giving can be tough on everyone's budgets—arrange to do secret Santa with friends or family (where you each pick a name out of a hat and only buy one nice gift), or agree on a spending limit that works for everyone.

- If you are short on money, get creative! Tutoring in something you are good at is a great way to generate extra income.

Not all debt is created equal.

- If you have debt—look at your interest rates. Credit card debt is the most urgent; student loans can wait because the interest rates are typically much lower.

- Student loan debt often has the lowest interest rates of all, and in some cases, it doesn't make sense to pay them off completely right away if that money could be earning more in the stock market or a high-yield savings account. Just make sure you continue chipping away at your monthly payments.

- Do whatever it takes to avoid late fees and finance/overdraft charges. In some cases, people spend more on fees than the majority of their actual purchases.

Slip up? Seven tips for getting out of debt and getting back on financial track:

1. **Face the facts.** Look at your finances line by line and figure out exactly how much you owe. Figure out exactly how much money you have coming in (income, reimbursements from work, IOUs, side jobs) and calculate the difference. That's the debt amount—the part you will need to get creative with.

2. **Prioritize your debt.** Create a plan for paying off debt with the highest interest rates first. For example, credit card debt is by far the worst, whereas student loans can wait.

3. **Cut back to only essential expenses.** Know that it won't be forever, but commit to at least two weeks of bare-bones spending. Those two weeks will be hard, but they are the most important if you want to start breaking your bad spending habits.

4. **Generate additional sources of income.** Tutoring in something you are good at is a great way to get some extra income. Less flexible but more reliable would be actually getting a second job. Ask for help from family (if that is available to you), especially if it means not spiraling into further debt because of exorbitant interest rates.

5. **Figure out how to pay yourself back.** Getting out of credit card debt will feel great—and that should be your first priority. But it is every bit as important to strategize and take action toward restocking your emergency fund and other savings accounts too.

6. **Reset your financial goals;** plan for the future. Make sure you aren't just playing defense when it comes to personal finance. Reset your goals (and readjust as necessary depending on what is realistic). Make a plan for saving up for things you will remember buying and doing—like traveling—that are aligned with your values.

7. **Reflect on what you've learned.** Arguably the most important step: look at what got you into debt and take action so it doesn't happen again.

It is never too late.

The most important thing I want to tell you about money is that you *can* get a handle on it. If you are looking for a place to start, I suggest the following:

1. **Admit your fears and flaws.** What are you afraid of? What are your biggest financial weaknesses? What do you avoid when it comes to managing your money? *(Check out the exercise later in this chapter called The Emotional Side of Money.)*

2. **Raise your Awareness.** What is your current state of affairs? How much money do you have in the bank? How much debt? What is your monthly income and outflow? *This chapter also includes a Four-Step Budget exercise to help you get this figured out.*

3. **Start somewhere.** At the very least, sign up for Mint.com so that you know where your money is going. Next step? Set up a short-term savings account and start having $50 automatically deposited every month for an emergency fund.

EXERCISE: FINANCIAL VALUE CHAINS

By understanding the values that underlie your financial goals, you will be much more likely to spend your money in ways that increase your overall happiness. Getting to the root of your values will also help you develop a framework for making financial decisions in the future.

It can be challenging to connect "stuff" with values. For the value chain exercise below, think of two things you want to buy or save money for (for example, travel or a big purchase).

When considering each big purchase or financial goal, ask "What does this provide?" or "Why is this important to me?" several times until you uncover the underlying values.

Examples:

• **Save for Retirement >** Security > Travel > Freedom to do whatever I choose > Ability to support my family, give back to the community

• **Upgrade my wardrobe >** Look professional at work > Feel more confident > Have great energy and presence every day

Value chain #1:

Item to buy or save for:

_____

Why is that important to you?

_____

Why is that important to you?

_____

Why is that important to you?

_____

Why is that important to you?

_____

Value chain #2:

Item to buy or save for:

_____

Why is that important to you?

_____

Why is that important to you?

_____

Why is that important to you?

_____

Why is that important to you?

_____

DEEP DIVE: ARE YOU CLOGGING YOUR FINANCIAL ARTERIES?

"The chief cause of failure and unhappiness is trading
what you want most for what you want now."
—Zig Ziglar

Crisp, sugary-sweet bacon. Hot, deliciously salty French fries. Food so mischievously tasty that you close your eyes as you savor those few seconds of blissful indulgence. So bad... but OH. SO. GOOD.

Most of us know what foods are particularly bad for us, but at times we still fall into the trap of short-term pleasure at the expense of long-term health (we are, after all, only human). We know that fatty, greasy foods corrode and clog our arteries. But the catch is that they do it slowly. If there were instant "artery clogged!" flags or side pains for every French fry consumed, it might be easier to say no. But instead, we say yes—hoping that in 30 years our arteries won't be *that* bad.

So how conscious are you when it comes to spending money? How are your short-term habits contributing to your long-term goals? Are you clogging your financial arteries for the sake of fleeting indulgences?

We all have our financial weak spots. Here are some seemingly innocuous habits that may be slowly clogging your financial arteries:

- Regularly purchasing items you don't need or that you don't use.

- Spending money before you've earned it ("I will be rich one day" or "I have a big paycheck coming, so I will spend as though I have it already").

- Spending large portions of your income or spending excessively on things that don't ultimately enhance your quality of life (for example: spending $100 on drinks at the bar. Was it really necessary?).

- Letting cable or cell phone companies overcharge you because you don't pay attention to your bills before paying them.

• Justifying purchases you know you shouldn't make by saying "I'll figure out how to pay for it later."

This is by no means a comprehensive list. It is meant to get you thinking.
What spending (or nonsaving) habits of yours are *not* contributing to a
healthy financial future?

_____

_____

_____

_____

And in what areas should you give yourself credit for building a strong
financial foundation?

_____

_____

_____

_____

For many of us, principles of healthy eating are easier to conceptualize
than healthy spending. So the next time you find yourself about to make
a stupid financial decision—yes, you heard me, stupid—stop and ask
yourself what the nutritional equivalent would be. Ten doughnuts? A
bucket of Kentucky Fried Chicken? A quarter pounder with bacon? And
then ask: is it still worth it? Or to reference Ziglar, are you trading what
you want most (for example, financial health and security) for what you
want right now?

ADVICE FROM COLLEGE GRADUATES

*Figure out your finances first. All too often we graduate, get a
job, and just assume that it'll all figure itself out. It's easy to get
tricked into thinking that you are making a lot of money because most
of us in college were not pulling in these kind of paychecks, but with
more money comes more expenses, like rent, cable, utilities, and food
which all tend to be much more costly than you think.*
—Vanessa M., USC

*That "thing" that's keeping you awake with excitement at night
probably isn't your next fat paycheck in and of itself, but the freedom
that comes with that paycheck. Aim for the freedom, not the check.*
—Eve Ellenbogen, Binghamton University (SUNY)

*AVOID CREDIT CARD DEBT!!! You may have the money
today to pay for the things that you put on your credit cards,
but the job market is so volatile, that things can change in the
blink of an eye. There is nothing more stressful than being out of work,
and missing payments and watching as your credit score is
lowered each day. That will haunt you for a long time.*
—Kristi R., St. Edward's University

*After saving frantically for years, I realized, "You can't
take it with you!" Learn how to live for today.*
—Ginny B., Long Island University

*Don't consistently borrow money from your parents. When
you're first getting set up, it's all right to borrow money ... how else
would you do it? But as soon as you can, cut the umbilical cord. For
me, my relationship with my mother has improved because
money is never a topic between us. I love having my own
money and not needing to rely on someone else.*
—Alison H., Bard College

DEEP DIVE:
LITTLE WHITE FINANCIAL LIES

You might be perfectly rational when it comes to spending money. But *juuust* in case you're not, let me share a little story about my coffee habit, then tell you how it relates to the little white lies we tell ourselves when spending money.

A little backstory on my love for coffee and how I talk to myself like a crazy person

One day I'm driving to work. I'm in a great mood. I approach Starbucks, which much to my chagrin AND my delight is directly en route to my office. My internal debate begins: "Should I go?" "No! Make a latte at work." "But I want Starbucks!" "You work at Google, land of the espresso machine! Don't you DARE pull over."

I veer off at the last minute. I *deserve* an iced latte. I've worked hard and it's hot outside. I get to the register. I also buy a breakfast sandwich. My total comes to $6.40. "No biggie, I mean, I would have spent at least $15 on brunch with friends anyway." "But it's Tuesday!" "Fine—then I'll make up for it over the weekend."

Do you think I made up for it that weekend? Definitely not. In fact, I rubbed it in my conscientious frugal-self's face by visiting Starbucks three times in one day! I visited Starbucks 146 times in the last year for a total of $889. Ouch.

I get that I'm talking about Starbucks here. A small purchase, given that I could be impulse-buying flat-screen TVs. But I don't think it matters—I think the white lies we tell ourselves are similar on purchases big and small. Below are three big ones of mine, along with some strategies for refuting them.

WHITE LIE #1: THE COUPON MENTALITY—IT'S OKAY THAT I SPENT $X BECAUSE I *COULD* HAVE SPENT $Y.

Example: It's okay that I bought a $500 TV I didn't need. It was on SALE.

Why We Tell the Lie: It makes us feel better. We spend money we probably shouldn't, then reassure ourselves by focusing on how much more we could have spent in some hypothetical scenario.

How to Counterbalance: When you notice yourself engaging in the "coupon mentality"—offer up a counter argument. On the Starbucks example, I've learned to remind myself "but you could have also made coffee at home for FREE."

WHITE LIE #2: I'VE EARNED IT! (OVER, AND OVER, AND OVER AGAIN)

Examples: I can buy this new pair of shoes—I've EARNED it. I've also earned an amazing meal, $50 worth in drinks with friends, and a new haircut. And my 3 times per day Starbucks habit.

Why We Tell the Lie: Because we want to reward ourselves for working so hard! Totally justifiable. But how many times have you "earned" what you are spending money on? I am all for spending money on things that make you happy, and for celebrating your hard work. We work so that we can enjoy our lives. Just be careful about how often you use this excuse. Have you really earned the 100th thing on your credit card statement?

How to Counterbalance: If you are working and saving money, that definitely earns you some splurge/reward purchases. Plan them in advance. Make sure that your "I've earned it" purchases aren't impulse buys—that they are items or experiences you really want. Another tried-and-true trick that your parents might have used when you were growing up: count the value of the item you are considering in work hours. These shoes cost two hours; this TV costs one week. Is it still worth it? If so, and you have the money, go for it!

WHITE LIE #3: IT'S FINE THAT I OVERSPENT—
I WILL TOTALLY MAKE UP FOR IT LATER.

Examples: I'll order this $50 item online (during the week) and go out to one less dinner this weekend.

Why We Tell the Lie: It is the true procrastinator in all of us—why pay now or hold ourselves back today when we can just make up for it later? The catch here is that by the time "later" rolls around, we've conveniently forgotten about the IOU we made with ourselves, which inevitably catches up with us (and our credit card bills) later.

How to Counterbalance: Work in the other direction—save your money first, then spend it once you've earned it. Don't make promises to yourself that you know you won't keep. When you find yourself saying "I'll make up for it later" pause for a second and ask yourself again, "Will I really?" If you are genuinely committed to making a trade-off in future spending for a purchase now, that's great—find a way to hold yourself accountable. Maybe even stick an IOU to your bathroom mirror as a reminder of how much less you should be spending over the weekend or on next month's purchases.

Your Turn to Fess Up: What are some of the little white lies you tell yourself when spending money? What are some reminders that will help you counterbalance them?

_____

_____

_____

EXERCISE: FINANCIAL GOAL BRAINSTORM

Goals are specific, measurable objectives that you want to achieve by a certain time. While some goals are solely money-based (save $10,000 by the time I'm 25), most are more general. Many life goals have a financial component (like buying a car or going to graduate school). The purpose of this exercise is to brainstorm as many goals as you can for each category; give yourself a range of fun, adventurous, and serious goals. For each goal, estimate the cost or dollar amount needed. You may want to continue where you left off with the goal brainstorm from the first chapter.

For each time period below, brainstorm goals around purchases, earnings, and savings. For example:

1. **Outgoing:** sign-up for a a yoga/river-rafting retreat during the summer at a cost of $1,000.
2. **Incoming:** generate extra income by coaching clients outside of work for an amount of $200/month.
3. **Saving:** increase my 401(k) contribution to 16% of my salary (up from 15%) OR save an extra $100 for my emergency fund.

6-month goals:

1. **Outgoing** (do or buy): _____

    at a cost of $ _____

2. **Incoming** (earn): _____

    at an amount of $ _____

3. **Save:** _____

    at an amount of $_____

1-year goals:

1. Outgoing (do or buy): _____

at a cost of $ _____

2. Incoming (earn): _____

at an amount of $ _____

3. Save: _____

at an amount of $_____

2- to 5-year goals:

1. Outgoing (do or buy): _____

at a cost of $ _____

2. Incoming (earn): _____

at an amount of $ _____

3. Save: _____

at an amount of $_____

Final step—narrow it down:

Read back through all of the goals you brainstormed above and **circle 3** to start working on based on the following questions:

• Which goal are you most **excited** about?

• Which one would have the biggest **impact**?

• Which one would be your **quickest win**?

EXERCISE: THE EMOTIONAL SIDE OF MONEY

Money is like food—we all have our weak spots. Some of us spend money emotionally. Some live in fear about money. Some have no fear! It is important to identify what your unique financial strengths and weaknesses are so you can start to address them and move toward financial freedom.

The purpose of this exercise is to examine your beliefs and emotions toward money so you can see how they may be affecting your saving and spending habits, and identify areas for improvement.

What is important to you about money?

_____

_____

_____

_____

_____

What emotions do you associate with money?

_____

_____

_____

_____

_____

What lessons did you learn about money from your family growing up ("good" or "bad"), both directly and from observation?

_____

_____

_____

_____

_____

In what ways do you manage money well?

_____

_____

_____

_____

What are some specific ways you could manage your money better?

_____

_____

_____

_____

Describe your ideal financial picture. How are you making money? How are you managing it? How are you spending it?

_____

_____

_____

_____

What area of financial management or spending concerns you most?

_____

_____

_____

_____

What one action could you take today to improve in this area?

_____

_____

_____

_____

My hope for all of us

What I want most for myself, for my friends, and for all of you is to see money as a source of freedom, not imprisonment. Of empowerment, not guilt or shame. Of conscious choices, not feelings of frustration or ignorance. No matter where you are starting from today, I know that you can do it.

Forget for a minute about how much money you have. I wish I could look you square in the eyes, but for now just hear me say: you are priceless, no matter what your bank statement says. You are smart, creative, and resourceful. There is nothing you can't figure out. Even this. *Especially this.*

EXERCISE: THE FOUR-STEP BUDGET

Detailed budgets can be difficult to create and even more challenging to maintain since they seem to stretch over what seems like a long period of time (at least one month) with lots of moving parts (most budgets have dozens of categories like shopping, groceries, utilities, etc.). To top it off, unplanned vacations or big purchases can throw the whole thing out of whack and leave you feeling discouraged and disorganized.

Enter the four-step budget. You might find it easier to break your budget down into three manageable chunks: income, outgoing must-have expenses, and outgoing nice-to-have expenses. Then you are left with an allowance that you can spend however you choose. This process is much simpler than trying to remember specific budget amounts for dozens of areas. (You can find an online spreadsheet version of this exercise in the Templates section of my website at LifeAfterCollege.org.)

How to calculate your monthly spending allowance:

1. **Add the take-home amount of your paychecks** (and any other sources of income) within a given month to get your total income.

2. **Add up your essential expenses** (rent, bills, taxes, insurance, gas, and groceries; don't forget to include savings in this category!).

3. **Add up your nice-to-have expenses** (things you really like to do/have each month but ultimately could live without, like coffee, personal grooming, and other recurring purchases).

4. **Subtract the total** from steps two and three from the total in step one to get your monthly spending allowance.

1. Step One: Monthly Income

Source: _____ $ _____

Source: _____ $ _____

Source: _____ $ _____

TOTAL: $_____

2. Step Two: Essential Expenses

Source: _____ $ _____

Source: _____ $ _____

Source: _____ $ _____

TOTAL: $_____

3. Step Three: "Nice-to-Haves"

SSource: _____ $ _____

Source: _____ $ _____

Source: _____ $ _____

TOTAL: $_____

4. Step Four: Monthly Allowance Calculation

Total from Step One: $_____ – (minus) Total from Step Two:

$_____ – (minus) Total from Step Three: $_____ =

Monthly Allowance: $ _____

EXERCISE: AN ALTERNATIVE TO THE SIMPLE BALANCE SHEET— WEEKEND BUDGETS

If I were to graph my spending over the course of a week, I would see a graph that looks like a mountain range—low, low, low Monday through Friday followed by a HUGE spike on Saturday and Sunday.

After holding back all week (save for a few online book purchases), my credit card explodes into the retail world on weekends, spending on breakfast, lunch, dinner, clothes, movies, drinks, you name it. Sound familiar? It might if you are used to working and laying low during the week, then splurging on weekends.

Enter the weekend budget.

If you have trouble tracking and following a monthly budget, experiment with a weekend budget instead. You may find it easier to break your budget down into smaller chunks of time.

Try the following formula for determining your weekend budget:

1. Complete steps 1–4 in the previous exercise to determine your Monthly Spending Allowance.

2. Divide the remaining amount by four. This is your weekend budget. Spend on whatever you would like each weekend as long as you stay within this amount. If it helps, take that amount out of the bank in cash and distribute that across your weekend activities.

In addition to more closely monitoring the money you spend on weekends, make a point to brainstorm fun things to do with friends that don't cost a lot of money (bike rides, hiking, volunteering, cooking dinner instead of going out, etc.).

DEEP DIVE: LIVING CREATIVELY

*"All the breaks you need in life wait within your imagination,
Imagination is the workshop of your mind, capable of
turning mind energy into accomplishment and wealth."*
—**Napoleon Hill,** Author of *Think and Grow Rich*

Life takes creativity. Solving problems takes creativity. Seeing the positive side of failures and setbacks takes creativity. I can't think of an area of life that *doesn't* take creativity.

So how can you practice living with creativity? It starts with curiosity. Think of some current challenges in your life. Examples might include feeling tired, wanting to lose weight, being worried about finances. List them first as problems, then take some time to turn them into questions (it helps to actually write them down). How can I increase my energy? How can I lose weight? How can I make extra income?

Reframing issues as questions invites your creative side to participate in the conversation. Even if you don't have the answers right away, your brain has an assignment—something to chew on rather than worry about.

This worked particularly well for me one summer; after purchasing a number of plane tickets in the same month, I knew I would be about $1,000 short of being able to pay my credit card bill. I was really concerned about going into credit card debt and didn't know how I would come up with the money.

So I started by expressing my concern as a question: How can I make $1,000 to pay my credit card bill? I brainstormed a list of things I could do, narrowed it down, and started doing HTML/CSS/Dreamweaver tutoring as a side job. Once I had a potential solution, I turned my question into a clearly stated goal: "Make $1,000 doing web tutoring by August 1." It worked, and I now feel infinitely more creative when it comes to solving financial issues.

EXERCISE: LIVING CREATIVELY

Make a list of problems or challenges you are facing at the moment (the list doesn't just have to be about money):

_____

_____

_____

_____

Now choose one or two problems (pick ones that seem hardest to solve) and rephrase them as questions:

1. _____

    _____

    _____

2. _____

    _____

    _____

Brainstorm: what are some potential answers or ideas for the questions you wrote above?

1. _____

    _____

    _____

2. _____

    _____

    _____

DEEP DIVE: CRAIGSLIST AS AN EXTRA INCOME DARTBOARD

Looking for some extra income but can't seem to think of a way to get it without exhausting yourself at a second job? Try putting some of your talents to use with the Craigslist-as-Dartboard approach. It involves some high-tech trial and error.

7 steps to generate extra income through Craigslist:

1. **Browse the services section** ("lessons & tutoring" is a good subset within services to start with).
2. **Keep a list of any services that sound fun to you** (and that you might be qualified to do), like tutoring or dog walking.
3. **Bookmark or copy posts you like into a separate document.** Note what you like about them (clearly written, interesting to read) and how much people are charging for these services.
4. **Narrow your list to two or three things you would be willing to try.** Write a post for each of those areas.
5. **Post and wait** to see if you get any responses!
6. **If you start or complete a job** and you don't like it, treat it as a learning experience.
7. **Change direction** altogether or tweak your offering to be more specific.

List some activities (keep it legal, please!) that could help you generate extra income:

_____

_____

Note: _If you don't have the time or energy to generate money through services like tutoring, remember that selling things like clothes, furniture, and old electronics on Craigslist or eBay can also be a great way to earn extra cash._

DEEP DIVE: REWARD GOALS

When I was 20 years old I set a very specific goal. I filled up an entire page of my journal with the following: "Five years from now, on October 9 (my birthday), I will buy myself a diamond right-hand ring worth at least $3,000."

Oh, the frivolity! I set a number of other more serious goals at the time, but this one was important because it symbolized independence, indulgence, and a reward for what I knew five years down the line would be a job well done.

About one year after setting my goal, writing it down, and manifesting my vision by cutting out pictures from magazines, I realized I hadn't actually taken any practical steps to make it a reality. So I set up a separate savings account and had money direct-deposited once a month to start building this fund. No matter what, I refused to cash out to pay for other things (including the purchase of my condo or paying off my credit card bill).

Once a goal has had five years to simmer and solidify, it *means* something. And writing something so specific made me steadfast in my resolve to stick to it and reward myself, no matter how frivolous it seemed at times.

Actually, the fact that I saved a little bit at a time over such a long period made it seem less frivolous because I earned that money and wasn't paying for the ring with borrowed debt. It taught me the value of automatic saving, and seeing that I will not be spending my retirement savings anytime soon, it gave me something to look forward to.

Benefits of working toward a reward goal:

1. It will reinforce the structure and benefits of sound financial planning while giving you something fun to look forward to.

2. It feels so much more gratifying to earn an expensive gift or trip

through regular, consistent saving rather than buying it on credit.

3. It's much more exciting than saving for retirement and definitely has a faster turnaround time. Just make sure your first priorities are still retirement and your emergency savings account; saving for a reward goal without these systems defeats the purpose.

Steps to create your own long-term reward goal:

1. **Identify something meaningful to you**; something that is rewarding, exciting, and outside of your comfort zone for what you might normally do or buy.

2. **Write a time-bound goal with the dollar amount attached.** (Example: In January 2012 I will purchase an airline ticket to Africa for a 3-week safari, at a total cost of $X,000.)

3. **Divide your target dollar amount by the number of months from now until your goal's target date.**

4. **Start a separate high-yield savings account for your goal.** Keep this separate from your everyday checking and savings accounts.

5. **Set up a recurring, automatic deposit of $X/month** (based on your earlier calculation) from your regular checking account; I suggest a few days after the first of the month. This allows your new savings account to take on a life of its own and grow without you having to pay attention to it every month.

What are some reward goals you might consider saving up for?

Stretch yourself—have some fun here! Don't limit yourself just to what you think is affordable right now. Saving a little bit at a time goes a long way.

1. _____

2. _____

3. _____

4. _____

5. _____

6. _____

7. _____

8. _____

9. _____

10. _____

11. _____

12. _____

13. _____

14. _____

15. _____

TWO CENTS FROM TWITTER

What's your philosophy when it comes to saving and/or spending money? Best tip?

@LMSandelin Depriving yourself completely is unrealistic—you work hard for that money, but use it for something worthwhile.

@doniree Know your priorities! My new clothes budget? Minimal. Travel? First thing saved for once my responsibilities are met.

@davidstehle Save and invest more than you spend. Only spend money you have today, not money you expect to have tomorrow. Want more? Work harder.

@MeganLoghry SAVE SAVE SAVE SAVE. My best advice is to keep living like a broke college kid even when you aren't anymore.

@ryanstephens Track your money. Save more than you think you need. Spend consciously, but treat yourself to things you're REALLY passionate about.

@JReid_DevCab Money, unfortunately does make the world go round . . . spend as little as you can until you have too much!

NOTABLE QUOTES

*Don't tell me where your priorities are. Show me where
you spend your money and I'll tell you what they are.*
—James W. Frick

A penny saved is a penny earned.
—Benjamin Franklin

*The poor, the unsuccessful, the unhappy, the unhealthy
are the ones who use the word tomorrow the most.*
—Robert Kiyosaki

*You can only become truly accomplished at something you love. Don't
make money your goal. Instead, pursue the things you love doing, and
then do them so well that people can't take their eyes off you.*
—Maya Angelou

*Invest three percent of your income in yourself
(self-development) in order to guarantee your future.*
—Brian Tracy

*Experience taught me a few things. One is to listen to
your gut, no matter how good something sounds on paper.
The second is that you're generally better off sticking with
what you know. And the third is that sometimes your
best investments are the ones you don't make.*
—Donald Trump

You aren't wealthy until you have something money can't buy.
—Garth Brooks

*Of the billionaires I have known, money just brings out
the basic traits in them. If they were jerks before they had
money, they are simply jerks with a billion dollars.*
—Warren Buffett

*You have not lived a perfect day, even though you have
earned your money, unless you have done something for
someone who will never be able to repay you.*
—Ruth Smeltzer

*Ordinary riches can be stolen, real riches cannot. In your soul are
infinitely precious things that cannot be taken from you.*
—Oscar Wilde

Being rich is having money, being wealthy is having time.
—Margaret Bonnano

*So many people spend their health gaining wealth,
and then have to spend their wealth gaining health.*
—A. J. Reb Materi

*Wealth is a tool of freedom, but the pursuit of
wealth is the way to slavery.*
—Frank Herbert

*What's money? A man is a success if he gets up in the morning
and goes to bed at night and in between does what he wants to do.*
—Bob Dylan

RECOMMENDED READING

Rich Dad, Poor Dad: What the Rich Teach Their Kids about Money—That the Poor and Middle Class Do Not!
Robert Kiyosaki

Your Money or Your Life: 9 Steps to Transforming Your Relationship with Money and Achieving Financial Independence
Joe Dominguez and Vicki Robin

The Money Book for the Young, Fabulous & Broke
Suze Orman

Get a Financial Life: Personal Finance in Your Twenties and Thirties
Beth Kobliner

The Total Money Makeover: A Proven Plan for Financial Fitness
Dave Ramsey

Naked Economics: Undressing the Dismal Science
Charles Wheelan

The Wall Street Journal Guide to Understanding Money and Investing
Kenneth M. Morris

Think and Grow Rich
Napoleon Hill

I Will Teach You to Be Rich
Ramit Sethi

The Complete Idiot's Guide to Personal Finance in Your 20s and 30s
Sarah Young Fisher and Susan Shelly

ONLINE MONEY MANAGEMENT TOOLS

Mint.com

Mint pulls financial information from all of your accounts (for example: checking, savings, credit card, investments, mortgage); shows spending trends, allows you to create and manage budgets and sends weekly or monthly financial summaries via e-mail. You can also text Mint to receive an instant update on your account balances, or download their handy mobile app.

CreditKarma.com

Allows you to check your credit score for free as often as you like, track your credit scores over time and get credit advice.

AnnualCreditReport.com

Allows you to generate a free credit report from all three of the major credit reporting agencies once a year. Note: You have to pay extra if you want to see your credit score.

SmartyPig.com

A "social savings" account that allows you to set up savings accounts for specific goals and share accounts with friends.

JustThrive.com

Also similar to Mint.com, Thrive brings all your credit card, checking, savings, retirement, and investment accounts into one place so you can "easily see what you have, what you owe, and where you can grow."

BankRate.com

Financial calculators for everything from retirement to taxes to auto loans and debt management.

4.Home

He is the happiest, be he king or peasant,
who finds peace in his home.
—Johann Wolfgang von Goethe

SECOND TO THE OFFICE, YOU PROBABLY SPEND A BIG chunk of your time at home. Whether you live alone or with roommates, it is important that you live in a place you can enjoy—or at the very least tolerate.

If you live in a place that feels dirty and cluttered, chances are that other areas of your life could use improvement too. By focusing on creating a relaxing physical environment, you will give yourself the space you need to unwind and recharge at the end of each day and each week.

This chapter is about:

- **Navigating life with roommates**
- **Making the most of your living space**
- **Quick tips for cleaning without too much hassle**

JENNY'S TIPS

Make smart investments—furnishing an apartment can add up faster than you might think.

- One word: Craigslist. Do not buy new if you haven't exhausted the used furniture market—it is just not worth it.

- If you are going to invest in something, invest in your bed (mattress, comforter, sheets, and pillows). You spend almost a third of each day in bed—make it comfortable.

- Pictures of friends and family go a long way when personalizing a new space. Buy cheap frames and add a few pictures to your room and common areas.

- It may take time to personalize your apartment—that is okay. If you try to accessorize or furnish all at once you will go broke and miss an opportunity to collect more meaningful (and interesting) items later on.

- If you are moving in with a new roommate, be clear about who is buying what. Going in on a couch is like going in on a dog—someone will end up keeping it when you go your separate ways.

- If you do purchase a big item with a roommate, make sure you are okay with buying out their half (or vice versa) or selling it when it is time to move.

Welcome to your new home life: navigating bills, roommates, and rent.

- If you move home after graduation, try not to stay for TOO long—there is something to be said for getting out on your own and creating a new independent life for yourself.

- Make sure you give a friend or nearby family member a spare key. You WILL lock yourself out at some point.

- Pay your rent on time. You might need your landlord to write a letter of recommendation for you someday if you are bidding on an apartment in a competitive market.

- If you are apartment hunting in a competitive market, show up BEFORE the open house starts. Bring your checkbook and a "personal file" with a bio, financial summary, credit report, and generic application. Potential landlords will love it!

- Before you move in, take pictures of the entire apartment. They will help you get your security deposit back when you move out (so you can show any preexisting damage).

- Be careful about living with good friends. It can put unexpected strains on your friendship; plus, then you lose your outlet for complaining about typical roommate issues.

- Paying bills on time is hard enough. Throw in roommates and bills become an even bigger beast to track and pay on time. Have a conversation up front about how you will pay bills in a way that works for everyone, and be clear about what you will do if someone is late.

- Spending on groceries adds up, especially if you buy things that perish quickly. Set a limit before you go grocery shopping and don't go when you're hungry!

- If you aren't naturally inclined to inviting friends over, do it anyway. It is good motivation to clean up your place, it is social, and it can be a fun opportunity to introduce people from different social circles.

Tips and tricks to help organize your house:

- Paper grocery bags make great recycling bins.

- Keep a stationery drawer with spare thank-you notes, notepads, and office supplies.

- Keep a little bowl or hook by the door for your keys so they don't get lost.

- If you have a roommate (or several), invest in a small vertical sorter for your mail. Each of you should have a section. Keep it by the front door or wherever you pick up your mail.

- Keep a recycling bin near your mail sorter so you can get rid of junk mail (like catalogs and coupons) as you are going through the rest of your mail.

- Keep a set of Post-Its in your bedside stand. If you think of things late at night that you don't want to forget, write them on a Post-It and stick it on your bedroom door or bathroom mirror so you see it as a reminder in the morning.

- Store an extra set of sheets, blankets, and towels in case you ever have someone crash at your place. If you can't (or don't want to) store a full set, at least have the basics: a pillow, a blanket, and a bath towel.

- Keep a drawer with scissors, Post-Its, tape, and an extra set of AA and AAA batteries. You'll need them all from time to time.

- Keep a flashlight handy and know where to find it. You never know when you might lose power, and fumbling around your house looking for it in the dark will not be easy.

- Keep shoes in their shoeboxes, and if there is no picture make a note on the box about what is in there. It makes it much easier to stack and store shoes, and adds a whole new level of order to your closet.

- Use a space heater instead of your built-in heating unit—it will save you money on your electric bill. Just be sure to turn it off before you leave the house or go to sleep.

- Buy stemless wine glasses—they break less easily than regular wine glasses.

- Renters or home insurance is worth paying for—it is relatively cheap and will protect you against fires or burglaries.

- Keep a can of Febreze and a toilet plunger in the bathroom. Your guests will thank you.

- Save energy; unplug kitchen appliances that you do not use often, and turn lights off when you leave the room.

- Stock your medicine cabinet with a few key essentials: aspirin,

Band-Aids, Neosporin, Tums, eye drops, calamine lotion, hydrogen peroxide, a gauze roll, and Sudafed and/or Claritin.

There are two constants in our home lives: laundry and dishes. You might as well get used to them!

- Doing dishes is fun! At least start telling yourself that—you have to do them anyway. Especially if you don't have a dishwasher, make a point to enjoy the hot water and the time you get to just stand there and think or reflect on the day.

- Buy a laundry sorter and use it; clothes are either dirty or they are not. Rather than leave them in a pile on the floor (we are all guilty of this from time to time), make a point to either throw them in the laundry or fold and put them away.

- If you don't have time to fold your laundry right after it is finished, at least pull out your shirts and pants and lay them flat to avoid wrinkles.

- Never put wool in the dryer! You'll end up with clothing fit for a toddler. Put a Post-It on top of the washer with a list of the clothes that shouldn't go in the dryer.

- Keep a dry-cleaning bag near your laundry basket or buy a laundry sorter that has three sections: whites, darks, and dry cleaning.

- Use a lint-roller for cleaning your duvet-cover between washes.

- Old socks make great dust rags.

Be vigilant with clutter.

- Do not be afraid to throw things out. Pens that don't work, broken items, things you don't use, clothes you don't wear, and other useless things just add clutter and take up space.

• Hold clothing or book exchange parties with friends to get rid of things you don't want. Your trash might be someone else's treasure.

Other cleaning tips:

• Your place may get messy during the week, so straighten up as much as you can on weekends. If you don't, you will start living in so much mess that by the time you get around to cleaning it will be an all-day activity.

• Even though life after college can be financially tough, invest in a cleaning service, even if just once a month or once every three months. If they are good, they will likely clean in areas you've never seen and every surface will sparkle. It's a great investment—almost always worth the money.

• Clean out your refrigerator often. If you frequently find food that has gone bad, take it as a sign to stop buying as many perishable foods, or to start eating your leftovers. Learn how to make homemade soup and stew.

• Buy disposable cleaning wipes. They work great for countertops, sinks, mirrors, and coffee tables.

Some of my favorite feng-shui principles for decorating (contingent upon the size and layout of your place, of course):

• If you can, place a mirror opposite your window. It reflects light and makes any room seem more spacious.

• Don't set up a desk or chair in a way that leaves your back to the entryway of the room. Whenever possible, have your back to a wall and face the open room.

• Leave room on both sides of your bed. Keep a small bedside table on both sides in case you have company.

• Keep (visible) clutter out of the bedroom. Don't have too many books out, stacks of papers, or piles of clothes. Your bedroom should inspire feelings of peacefulness, calm, clean, and relaxation.

- On that note, any clocks in your bedroom should be silent (not ticking) and if digital, have a dimmer setting.

- If you do have small pockets of clutter, keep them away from your mirrors, which will make them appear twice as large.

- If you're like me and you can't keep real plants alive to save your life, keep an eye out for realistic looking fake plants (or *flants* as my brother calls them). They will add color and warmth to a room.

- Make a clear distinction between work spaces and rest spaces. For example: I don't keep a TV in my bedroom because that is a place I have designated for personal reflection, journal writing, reading, and unwinding before bed.

- I have also set a "no laptop in bed" policy. In fact, for a while I specifically chose not to have wireless Internet, so that the only place I can use the Internet when I'm at home is in the living room.

ADVICE FROM COLLEGE GRADUATES

Try living with both genders. It is a great way to mature as a person and learn how to work with the opposite sex, and a great way to meet and get advice on potential boy-/girlfriends. Finally, if you are in a bad situation get out immediately. Moving may seem like a pain, but it is worth it.
—**Adam M., Stanford University**

A fortune-teller's tip for predicting your future relationships with roommates: have a genuine conversation about living together, and then go with your instincts. Further, here's a little hard-learned advice: always leave the shared spaces cleaner than they were when you entered; when you're feeling generous, offer your roommate a sample of whatever delicious meal you're cooking; be sure to pay the bills as early as you possibly can. It's easy to skip out on the small stuff, but the small stuff is what turns your roommate into a good friend and what makes a "living arrangement" a home.
—**Eve Ellenbogen, Binghamton University (SUNY)**

There comes a point when you don't have to live like a college student any more. During college so many of us become accustomed to substandard living arrangements—whether lawn chairs in the living room or an absence of a kitchen table. Buy some real furniture (that you don't assemble) and start living like an adult. It's an exciting thing when you realize you a) don't HAVE to live like you did during college and b) you don't WANT to.
—**Sharalyn Hartwell, Utah State University**

Establish ground rules at the beginning of the year. Is there a set schedule for chores? If girl- or boyfriends regularly stay over, should they have to chip in for utilities? How late is too late to have people over? It's much easier to tackle these things before the problems arise, especially if you live in a house with a handful of people.
—**Teresa Wu, University of California, San Diego**

Home 133

DEEP DIVE: TIPS TO CONTROL CLOTHING CHAOS

I don't know about you, but I only actively wear about a third of the clothes in my closet. And that is probably a generous estimate. Here are 3 strategies that have kept me from having to do a major closet overhaul every year:

Put a donation bin in your closet.

Collect items on a daily basis (or as you try things on that you know you will never wear). When the bin gets full, take it to Goodwill (or any charity) for donation and benefit from a tax write-off. Don't forget to document your donations: either write a list with each item and its estimated value, or lay all your clothes on the table and take a photo before you donate them.

Try this rule: no new hangers!

Ever find yourself short of hangers, so you go buy ten more to accommodate your ever-growing clothing collection? This could go on forever if you don't take time to clear things out. With the "no new hangers" policy if you buy something new and want to hang it, something else in the closet has to go. (The hard part is resisting the urge to just stuff everything in drawers instead.)

Create an "on probation" section in your closet (or designate a drawer).

These are clothes that you can't bring yourself to throw away . . . yet. Review the section or drawer from time to time and if you haven't worn an item in the last two years (one year if you are really serious) throw it in the donation bin.

DEEP DIVE: SEARCHING FOR THE *RIGHT* ROOMMATE

Whether you live alone or with others, there may come a time when you need to look for a new roommate. Before you talk to friends or post a roommate wanted ad, take some time to get clear on exactly what you are looking for.

Here are some considerations to ask yourself about the type of roommate you're seeking:

- General personality type
- Level of cleanliness
- Level of social interaction (never home versus home with friends over all the time)
- Philosophy on pets, smoking, living with someone of the opposite sex

Questions you may want to ask potential roommates:

- Job/occupation, age
- What is your average weekday like? Average weekend?
- What are your hobbies/interests?
- What have you liked in past roommates?
- What are you looking for in this living situation?
- Are you a morning or night person?
- How do you feel about visitors? Do you have people over often?
- Are you in a serious relationship? If so, how much time do you estimate that person would spend here?
- What is your general cleanliness level and housecleaning approach?
- How often do you drink or smoke?
- (Consider also asking for references)

DEEP DIVE: CLEANING
SHORTCUT—SHINY SINKS

The following quote is from FlyLady.net, a cleaning/clutter and organization blogger. She is a big proponent of taking 5 minutes of your time to shine your kitchen and bathroom sinks.

Even if you don't do anything else, this will give your sinks (and the rooms they live in) an impression of being sparkly and clean—distracting your visitors from other messes you might not have time to clean up. It also gives you a sense of accomplishment, and might encourage you to spend another 5 minutes tidying up.

Flylady says:

"This is your first household chore. Many of you can't understand why I want you to empty your sink of your dirty dishes and clean and shine it, when there is so much more to do.
It is so simple. I want you to have a sense of accomplishment.
I just want to put a smile on your face. When you get up the next morning, your sink will greet you and a smile will come across your lovely face. I know how good it feels to see yourself in your kitchen sink. So each morning this is my gift to you. Even though I can't be there to pat you on the back, I want you to know that I am very proud of you. Go shine your sink!"
—FlyLady.net

There are many different types of cleaning wipes you can buy—all-purpose, wood, tile, and glass. They are cheap and work wonders on sinks and countertops. Keep a container of cleaning wipes under the sink in your kitchen and bathroom, and in less than 5 minutes you can get rid of all those toothpaste & water splashes, shine your sink and have your kitchen and bathroom looking brand new. It's amazing what a difference it makes!

EXERCISE: CLEAR YOUR CLUTTER

This exercise will help you identify the area in your house that most needs an overhaul, and will hopefully give you the push you need to start making that happen.

What area of your house or apartment feels the most cluttered and/or unorganized? What is the current state?

Personal example: My coffee table. It's not that big to begin with, and it seems to be constantly piled with papers, magazines, books, bills, and remote controls.

_____

_____

_____

What factors or behaviors contribute to the clutter?

Personal example: I dump all of my mail and papers on my coffee table when I get home from work. By the end of the week, I can barely see it!

_____

_____

_____

What would a one-time clean-up of this area involve? How much time do you think it would take? What could you do to make it more fun and/or reward yourself afterward?

Personal example: I could spend 30 minutes sorting the papers and filing my bills. I'd wipe down the coffee table and set the magazines out in a nice way. Once it is clean, I will reward myself by buying a new coffee-table book.

_____

_____

_____

What are one or two behaviors you can practice moving forward to keep this area from getting cluttered again?

Personal example: I could keep a file box and recycling bin closer to my front door so that my papers have a home before they reach the coffee table. I could also buy a nice table decoration so there is less room for clutter in the first place.

_____

_____

_____

How would it change the energy of your space to keep this area uncluttered?

Personal example: I would feel more relaxed when I get home from work and hang out in my living room. I wouldn't be staring at a pile of bills and papers that need to be cleaned, read, and dealt with.

_____

_____

_____

Now you have no excuse not to clear your clutter—you've identified the one area in your house that needs the most work, a way to do an overhaul to kick-start the clean zone, one or two key behaviors to keep it neat moving forward, and a compelling reason to stick to your clutter-free goal.

Just like any habit, keeping this area clear will take practice and commitment, but it will get easier over time. Try keeping the area clean for one week (despite any temptations to revert to your old habits) and see how you feel—my guess is that it will give you greater peace of mind than you might think!

EXERCISE: INSPIRED LIVING

Making an apartment feel like a home can seem like a lot of work, not to mention expensive. However, if you put some thought into the overall look you want to create and feelings you want to inspire, you can usually find ways to do it cheaply and with minimal effort. These questions will help you envision ways to make your place feel more personalized. I also recommend buying a few home-decorating magazines (or watching HGTV) and keeping a list of ideas that appeal to you.

How do you want to feel when you walk into your room or apartment?
Example: inspired, creative, relaxed, high-energy, fun, Zen-like

_____

_____

What are your favorite colors, fabrics, and shapes?
Dark or light, bright or subtle, soft or textured, round or hard-edged? Modern or traditional? Patterned or plain?

_____

_____

If you were to splurge on one statement piece for each room, what would it be?

Bedroom:_____

Living Room:_____

Other: _____

What are some of your favorite exotic places? What are your favorite souvenirs?

Example: the beach, Morocco, Japanese gardens, trinkets from market-places (especially of people dancing).

_____

_____

What are some of your favorite places you've stayed (including hotels, motels, hostels, and friend's houses)? What makes them special or appealing to you?

Example: modern hotels with bright colors and clean lines, bed and breakfasts that feel homey but not too old and flowery, houses that have lots of dark-wood furniture and big colorful bookshelves.

_____

_____

Ideas into action: What could you do to make your place more closely resemble the concepts you brainstormed above?

Example: paint my bedroom an earthy color (it's burnt-orange); buy nice-smelling candles; find a really bright pillow or piece of furniture; put up lots of pictures (even if they are in cheap frames).

1. _____

2. _____

3. _____

4. _____

5. _____

6. _____

TWO CENTS FROM TWITTER

How can someone make the most of their living space? Best advice for dealing with roommates?

@TandooriKnight Splurge on a good mattress, buy an exercise ball and dumbbells, learn to cook simple meals, clean = Zen.

@kristenbyers Be persistent when apartment hunting. Try to find a friend or relative to crash with while you look so that you don't feel rushed.

@Steve_Campbell Don't sweat the little things. There will be plenty of bigger things to fight about with your roommates.

@SJOgborn Don't make your bedroom your office! Get out and go somewhere to do work. Your bedroom should be for sleep and relaxing.

@laurenkgray Give roommates their space. Even the best of friends need time apart. Respect each others' stuff and ALWAYS ask to use things.

NOTABLE QUOTES

Law of Window Cleaning: It's on the other side.
—Unknown

I have been very happy with my homes, but homes really are no more than the people who live in them.
—Nancy Reagan

Decorate your home. It gives the illusion that your life is more interesting than it really is.
—Charles M. Schulz

He who wants to change the world should begin by cleaning the dishes.
—Paul Carvel

Housework is something you do that nobody notices until you don't do it.
—Author Unknown

It's possible to own too much. A man with one watch knows what time it is; a man with two watches is never quite sure.
—Lee Segall

Beauty in things exists in the mind which contemplates them.
—David Hume

Nor need we power or splendor, wide hall or lordly dome; the good, the true, the tender, these form the wealth of home.
—Sarah J. Hale

RECOMMENDED READING

150 Best Apartment Ideas
Ana G. Canizares

Design on a Dime: Achieve High Style on a $1,000 Budget
HGTV and Amy Tincher-Durik

Rules for Roommates: The Ultimate Guide to Reclaiming Your Space and Your Sanity
Mary Lou Podlasiak

Eliminate Chaos: The 10-Step Process to Organize Your Home and Life
Laura Leist and Adam Weintraub

Mission: Organization—Strategies and Solutions to Clear Your Clutter
HGTV and Amy Tincher-Durik

Organizing Plain and Simple: A Ready Reference Guide with Hundreds of Solutions to Your Everyday Clutter Challenges
Donna Smallin

Real Simple Solutions: Tricks, Wisdom and Easy Ideas to Simplify Every Day
Editors of Real Simple *Magazine*

Real Simple: The Organized Home
Editors of Real Simple *Magazine*

Style Statement: Live by Your Own Design
Carrie McCarthy and Danielle LaPorte

Bedroom Feng Shui
Clear Englebert

The Complete Idiot's Guide to Feng Shui
Elizabeth Moran and Master Joseph Yu

5.Organization

"Be steady and well ordered in your life so that
you can be fierce and original in your work."
—**Gustave Flaubert**

L IFE IS SO MUCH EASIER WHEN YOU HAVE IT ORGANIZED; you will think more clearly, become less forgetful, feel more productive, and get more done. When life gets chaotic, some of the first things to go are usually our trusty systems and processes. These techniques should help you create a sense of order and clarity so that you can focus on the big stuff—major priorities and thoughts—in a calm, clear-headed way.

Organization is really about NOT procrastinating—it is about doing things quickly, cleaning as you go, filing papers as they come in, and grouping small tasks together to save time. If you have the right systems in place and you make a concerted effort to do a little bit each day, you will feel much more organized and at peace with your environment.

This chapter is about:

- **Creating systems to organize things like appointments, birthdays, bills, and files**
- **Keeping contact information organized and accessible**
- **Protecting your digital files**
- **Prioritizing your time and automating routine tasks**
- **Capturing thoughts and ideas**

JENNY'S TIPS

A simple filing system is the key to a happily organized life.

- Label folders consistently across different organizing platforms, like browser bookmarks, desktop folders, paper folders, and e-mail folders. The benefit is that you always know where to find things, regardless of their format.

- Give your papers a home. Buy a portable file box; keep your bills and important documents in it. Some key folder categories to start with: receipts and warrantees for major purchases, medical, car, utility bills, credit card and bank statements, travel, investment and tax documents.

- Label your folders clearly so you know where to find important papers when you need them. Invest in a label-maker.

- A tip for keeping files neat: use one manila folder per hanging folder. Keep all of the plastic labels on the left- or right-hand side—it makes it easier for your eye to scan through.

- Keep a "to file" folder if you can't get into the habit of filing your bills and papers as soon as they come in. Go through the folder once a month.

- Toss utility bills, bank statements and paycheck stubs after one year. Hang onto big receipts, tax-return documents, and medical records.

In a world increasingly moving online and to our computers, organizing, and protecting electronic files is more important than ever.

- BUY AN EXTERNAL HARD DRIVE and back up your data! Pictures, music, documents—all of it. Set a recurring reminder to do this once a month, or at a frequency that works for you. You won't regret it. It might cost money up front, but you will get peace of mind in return. Just think of how upset you would be if your computer crashed (or got stolen) and you lost everything.

- Be vigilant about e-mail spam (whether it's for V1Agr$ or a newsletter you don't want). If you receive an unwanted e-mail, unsubscribe immediately and delete. Save yourself the annoyance of deleting the same thing over and over again.

- If you are not quite ready to unsubscribe from something like a mailing list, at least set up a filter when you receive the first mailing so you don't have to label or file each e-mail individually.

Stay organized with an online calendar:

- Create a calendar for tracking appointments, setting reminders and generally staying on top of things after college. I use Google Calendar because it is linked to my Gmail account and I can easily share events (or the entire calendar) with family and friends.

- In addition to tracking day-to-day events, you use your calendar to:

  - Set up monthly reminders to pay your rent and bills.

  - Set up reminders to schedule appointments.

  - Set up annually recurring events for birthdays and other important days to remember (like anniversaries).

  - In the settings, sign up for text or e-mail alerts to receive your daily agenda (or reminder alerts for specific events).

Miscellaneous tips and tricks:

- Always carry a notebook to write things down when you are on the go: ideas, phone numbers, shopping lists, to-do lists, etc. I swear by my little black Moleskine.

- A tip for packing clothes into a small suitcase: roll your shirts or underwear and stick them into your shoes or small crevices. Rolling shirts also helps avoid wrinkles.

- Keep a car emergency kit in your trunk: thick paper towels, road flares, a toolkit, jumper cables, bottled water, foil-wrapped power bars, and a bottle of engine oil. It also helps to keep a few dollar bills in case you pass an unexpected toll road, and a small tin for loose parking-meter change.

- Keep another box in the trunk of your car to hold and organize blankets, a change of clothes (for gym or work emergencies), and sports gear (like tennis racquets, a football, or a Frisbee).

- Dog-ear magazine articles as your read; when you are ready to throw the magazine out, rip out the articles you like and put them in a binder or folder for later reference.

- Sell books you will never read or reference again (or do a book exchange with friends). You might also want to check out BookCrossing.com, a site that lets you find and share books with others.

DEEP DIVE: WANT MORE SUCCESS AND WORK/LIFE BALANCE? LEARN TO PRIORITIZE.

Oftentimes when we're not living or performing up to our full potential, it's because our priorities are out of whack—or nonexistent. This often happens when we have so many things to do that we start with what's easiest or nearest (like e-mails) rather than on more strategic activities that will truly move us forward. It's like constantly playing defense without every switching to offense—it might keep us in the game, but it won't score us any points.

I'm guessing we're all guilty of obsessively hitting "refresh" on our e-mail inbox just to avoid a bigger, more intimidating project or life goal. By taking a few minutes each day to prioritize, you can minimize stress and increase your impact.

Common signs that you could benefit from resetting your priorities:

• You want to make a bigger impact at work.

• You want people to appreciate the work you do.

• You feel buried in e-mails and meetings, and you are constantly reacting or playing catch-up.

• You want more time to yourself outside of work.

• You want to spend the free time you have doing fulfilling things; things that make you happy.

There is only one fundamental prioritization question: what one change or action will have the biggest impact on my (work, life, project, success, finances, relationships)?

Some examples of this question manifested in work and life (with room for you to do some brainstorming):

Impact and development:

What 1 or 2 key behavior changes or performance improvements will have the biggest impact on my development and on my contribution to my team/company?

1. _____

2. _____

Project management:

What 1 or 2 tasks are critical to the success of my project this week?

1. _____

2. _____

Work/life balance:

What three activities are most important to my daily routine?

1. _____

2. _____

3. _____

Happiness:

What is **one** change I can make that will have the greatest impact on my happiness?

_____

We all know that e-mails, meetings, and busywork could fill 24 hours of every day, seven days a week. The people who succeed are not the ones who get every tiny task done or try to improve on every single weakness.

The people who succeed are the ones who focus their time and energy on the highest-impact, highest-priority activities and learn to say "no" or "you can wait" to the rest. As the saying goes, "Work smarter, not harder."

DEEP DIVE: HOW I STAY ORGANIZED

When I worked at the start-up company, the big joke was that I could read people's minds, and that I was "hiding 5 Jennys in there" (I credit this to my ninja-like organization skills). Suffice it to say that discovering (or creating) new organizational tactics is a passion of mine.

That said, I still have a long way to go. In no way have I totally mastered personal organization and productivity—for me, it's always a work-in-progress (especially as life gets more complex). I hope you will find value in some of the systems that work for me.

Schedule:

Google Calendar —I have three calendars that I can see all at once: one for work, one for personal events, and one for birthdays. On the birthday calendar, I set each event to last all day so it shows up at the top, and to recur annually. For really important birthdays, I also set an e-mail or text reminder one day or week in advance.

Appointments spreadsheet—I use this to track medical and car appointments. I record "last appointment" and "next due" along with key contact information for each provider (see the exercise at the end of this chapter to create your own).

E-mails:

Inbox— I use my e-mail as a to-do list. I do not subscribe to the "inbox to zero" philosophy if it means filing things I haven't finished or responded to, just so they are out of my inbox. When I complete an action, I archive the e-mail. If I know I won't take action for a while, I archive the e-mail and add the action as a task on my to-do list instead.

Enable "superstars" feature in Gmail— The superstars feature allows you to star e-mails with various symbols. I star an e-mail when I need to respond to a person (rather than handle a task or read a newsletter); I "super-star" with an exclamation mark when I feel like I'm overdue on my reply.

Labels— I make sure the labels match the folder names on my computer and the categories in my Google Bookmarks (which allows me to access my bookmarks from any computer). I name important labels with numbers first (example: 1—Family).

Capturing ideas, notes, tasks:

Small notebook—I carry a small black Moleskine with me for personal use—capturing to-do lists on weekends, shopping lists, blog ideas, contact information, and other notes when I'm on the go.

Work notebook—I primarily use this for taking meeting notes so that I'm not distracted by trying to take notes on my laptop. At the start of every week, I also place a big Post-It on the cover and draw a line down the middle. On the left I list key work priorities, on the right I list personal tasks. When the week is over or I finish everything, I stick the Post-It inside the notebook and label it with the date. *(You may also find TeuxDeux.com handy for tracking tasks on a weekly basis.)*

Online to-do list—I use Todoist.com, which is a great online tool that allows you to group tasks by projects. I use this when I get overwhelmingly busy or am working on a complex project. I also use it to track longer-term action items or things without a fixed deadline, otherwise I find that a simple pen, paper, and Post-It works better for me.

Other online "collection" buckets:

Google Docs—I keep Google Docs for collecting various pieces of information over time. For example: quotes, tips from mailing lists I subscribe to, and ideas for various projects I am working on. Each of those has its own document, which makes it really easy to find and store key information, especially because it is all in one place (not buried in my e-mail inbox).

Things to read later—For e-books or other lengthy articles, I tag them in Delicious as "read later."

(You can view my bookmarks at Delicious.com/jennyblake.)

Other offline "collection" buckets:

A folder called "To File"—This is where I stick bills and papers when I'm too lazy to file them in my file box. When the "to file" folder gets big (about every 3 months), I file everything at the same time.

Post-It notes by my bed and front door—I keep Post-It notes in several areas of my house for important next-day reminders.

Key Plate—Simple, but works like a charm: I keep a plate on the bookshelf by my front door to hold my keys. Which is why they are never lost (until I forget to take them and lock myself out!).

Your turn:

Brainstorm some organizational tactics that might help you get a better handle on the following areas.

1. Managing your schedule:

_____

2. Managing your e-mail inbox:

_____

3. Managing your bills and papers:

_____

4. Storing important information or ideas:

_____

5. Capturing ideas or tasks while on-the-go:

_____

DEEP DIVE: GET THE RIGHT NETWORKING SYSTEMS IN PLACE

Networking is most fun when you can connect with people naturally, but it can help tremendously to have effective systems in place to support those connections. After I attend an event (skip to step 3 for people I meet online), I usually go through the following 5 steps:

1. **File business cards and add people to social networks.** I store my business cards in a regular-sized binder that has special sheet protectors with individual slots for each card. I suggest writing the context in which you met the person on the back of their card, and one or two physical descriptors.

2. **Identify people to follow up with.** At any given event, there are usually 2 or 3 people I want to get to know better. I plug their names into my networking spreadsheet, which tracks people I want to have follow-up conversations with. That way I don't have to refer back to their business card any more—their information is easily accessible online (and stored in one place). I can also skim through it later and drop people a note if I haven't talked to them in a while.

3. **Add follow-up names to my to-do list.** One of my categories on my to-do list is called "Networking." I add tasks with the names and e-mail addresses of people I want to schedule for a follow-up call. As my coach Ruth-Ann points out, "it doesn't get done if it doesn't get scheduled."

4. **Make the call (via phone or Skype).** This is the fun part!

5. **Send a follow-up e-mail to say thank you** (and make a note on my spreadsheet if we mentioned talking again at some point).

DEEP DIVE: EVERYBODY NEEDS A KEEPERS FILE

I may be stating the obvious on this one. The painfully obvious. But it's so important to me that I feel compelled to make sure you are in the loop.

It's called a Keepers file, and everybody needs one. You'll know a "keeper" when you see it—it's an e-mail, tweet, or otherwise glowing note about you that makes you smile from ear to ear. The kind that makes your whole day, week, or month. Keepers are like gold nuggets that never lose their value. You'll know it's a Keeper because every time you read it, you feel energized, confident, and/or appreciated.

Your Keepers deserve a home. They are proof of how hard you've worked, the impact you've had—or maybe they just make you laugh. I began saving Keepers a few years ago when I started training new hires at Google (thanks to a tip from a more seasoned co-worker). As the e-mails came in, I would label them "Keepers" and read through the e-mail folder on rainy days when I needed a pick-me-up.

Now I've figured out a better system—every time a Keeper comes in, I copy and paste it into a Google Doc with the date and a note about who it came from. WOW. What a difference the new system has made! E-mails were a little tough to sift through—the Google doc is like a Keepers file on a quad-shot latte.

I don't read Keepers to be vain, and I don't reread them all that often. I read them when I need a reminder about the difference I made in someone else's life, or an accomplishment I am proud of. I read them when I've forgotten that I have so much to be thankful for. I hope you are doing yourself the favor of saving Keepers too.

ADVICE FROM COLLEGE GRADUATES

When I get into the habit of spending 15 minutes a day on something I feel GREAT. Whether it's 15 minutes cleaning, 15 minutes declutter-ing, or just 15 minutes organizing—it all makes for a pleasant mind.
—J.M., James Madison University

Focus on only one task at a time. Turn off Gchat, AIM, Skype, and forbid yourself from going on Facebook, YouTube, or Hulu until you're done with the task. E-mail should also always be closed unless you're actively checking it. Before you go to sleep, take a piece of paper and fold it over twice. Write down the top 5-10 things you need to accomplish the next day. You are NOT allowed to go on sites that distract you until you accomplish those 5-10 tasks.
—Jun Loayza, University of California, Los Angeles

My prioritizing system: do everything within 72 hours of when you get it. Break it down to components if it will take longer than that. The more time you spend procrastinating and putting it off, the less time you'll have to do it.
—Andrew Weitsman, University of Tulsa

Do what works for you. I like keeping a list of what needs to get done and doing the most important/challenging thing first (or when I'm operating at peak efficiency/alertness). This sets the tone for the rest of the day. OR you can do a few small tasks earlier in the day and build up momentum by crossing things off your list and tackle the big goal later in the day.
—Ryan Stephens, Texas Lutheran/Texas A&M

Have too many magazines? Keep binders for specific topics. For example: home decoration, recipes, etc. This keeps my magazine pile low.
—Megan S., Westmont College

DEEP DIVE: TIME MANAGEMENT TIPS FROM A SELF-EMPLOYED WORLD TRAVELER

by Colin Wright, ExileLifestyle.com

As a serial entrepreneur and world traveler (I run my businesses from a new country every four months... the readers of my blog vote on where I go next), I've got a lot of balls in the air at any given time, and keeping them flying instead of falling requires a great deal of discipline and more than a few creative solutions to common problems.

Here are three of the incredibly-simple-yet-incredibly-helpful practices that I make use of.

Batch processing

I do one specific type of activity all at once. So if I've got a bunch of e-mails to answer, I'll wait until I have about 10 and then answer them all at once. When I approach the task this way I'm able to get into the "answering e-mail zone" and knock them out quickly and with better content than if I were to do them one at a time, piecemeal, over the span of a day. Also, you don't interrupt as many other tasks using this method, which saves time and keeps you from getting out of the zone with whatever else you're working on.

The 80/20 principle

This involves reducing or removing from your life the 80% of tasks, objects, and people who only bring 20% of your total value and instead focusing on the things (the other 20%) that brings you 80% of your total value. In a lot of cases this means a drastic restructuring, but it also means that what you DO keep will get more of your attention, so you'll generally come out with a lot more than you started with.

Parkinson's Law

Parkinson's Law essentially states that the amount of time that you have to do something is the amount of time it will take to do it. Knowing this, I give myself artificial deadlines that I strictly hold myself to. Because of this, I can finish elaborate projects that have a three-month deadline in one week. It's funny what you can get done when you put the pressure on and focus.

DEEP DIVE: CREATE THE ULTIMATE REMINDER FILE

If you don't have a place to keep track of recurring appointments (medical or otherwise), you will always be scratching your head trying to remember when you are due—or forget about them completely. Below is a system for storing information about recurring appointments. (You can also find this template online on my website.)

STEP ONE:
Create a spreadsheet in Excel or Google Docs to track the items on the next page.

STEP TWO:
Even with a tracking spreadsheet, it can be hard to remember when you are due for your next appointment. Make sure to set reminders in your calendar for the appointment itself. If it's too far away, set a calendar reminder to call and make the next appointment (include the phone number in the reminder).

STEP THREE:
Add your doctor and dentist's phone numbers to your phone book. It will take the hassle out of making appointments.

TYPE OF SERVICE	COMPANY/NAME	PHONE NUMBER	LAST APPT	NEXT APPT
HEALTH				
Doctor				
Dentist				
Optometrist				
Other				
CAR				
Oil Change				
Minor Service				
Major Service				
Tire Alignment & Rotation				
Renew License				
OTHER				
Pet Appt.				

DEEP DIVE: GOING BEYOND THE TO-DO LIST

You might already keep a daily and/or weekly to-do list—here are a few others to help keep you organized.

Ideas:

Your ideas need to have a home. As David Allen explains in his book *Getting Things Done*, our brain is great at coming up with ideas, but terrible at storing and remembering them. Many of my best ideas come to me at night right before bed, so I keep a notepad on my nightstand. An ideas list is great because even if you don't want to act on it now, you can always return to the list later.

Big purchases:

Keep a list of big purchases: items that you know you want but can't afford right now, or that you want to think about for a little longer to make sure they are worthy of your hard-earned cash. The most effective way to use a "big purchases" list is to constantly reorder in terms of importance, which will help you focus on saving for those few things that are really important to you (instead of splurging on random big ticket items as you run into them).

IOUs:

Keep a spreadsheet with a list of monthly expenses, big purchases, and IOUs (both what people owe you and what you owe them). Keeping an IOU list is an important part of ensuring that your finances are up-to-date and accounted for. This should also include rebates and other things you are waiting for in the mail. And if you "borrow" money from one of your savings accounts to pay for something like a credit card bill, write yourself an IOU!

Your life checklist:

Arguably the most important list, your life checklist captures and reminds you of all your dreams, big and small, of what you want to do in this lifetime. (Skip to the Fun & Relaxation chapter to complete the life checklist exercise.)

Unanswered questions:

My dad and I have a little game we play called "drop the bucket." The analogy is that there is an empty bucket in your brain that represents an unanswered question. If you drop the bucket into the well of your brain (like a wishing well), when it's ready it will come back up with the answer.

So when you're looking for answers or ideas, write the questions down and "drop the bucket" and the answer will come up eventually. The point here is less about the game, and more about the notion that asking the right question is the hard part—once it's out there in the universe and you review it periodically over the course of days or weeks, your mind will begin to wrap around the question and give you some answers. Keep your unanswered questions list somewhere where you can see it, and make sure to review it frequently.

Another great list exercise involves turning stresses in your life into questions. "I can't pay my credit card bill" becomes "How can I pay $X of my credit card bill by July 1?" Another example: "I have so many meetings and e-mails I can't get my important projects done" becomes "How can I prioritize my tasks at work?

What are some unanswered questions you are currently facing?

- _____
- _____
- _____

EXERCISE: STOP/START/CONTINUE

Stop/start/continue is an exercise you can use in many areas of your life: work, leadership, and time management, to name just a few. For this chapter, brainstorm what behaviors you could stop, start, and continue to help you feel more organized at home and at work.

Stop:

For example: keeping pens that don't work; ignoring e-mails that I know I could respond to quickly; stacking papers instead of filing them away.

1. _____

2. _____

Start:

For example: answer e-mails the first time I open them (unless there is a major task required); buy a better file organizer to sit on top of my desk at work.

1. _____

2. _____

Continue:

For example: recycling junk mail the minute I get it; immediately unsubscribing from spam or e-mail newsletters I no longer want; carrying a notebook to capture ideas on the fly.

1. _____

2. _____

TWO CENTS FROM TWITTER

What's one technique you use to stay organized and/or manage your time effectively?

@kristenbyers I cram so much work into my day, I make sure to schedule relaxation time when I can to watch a movie, play video games, etc.

@freddylee Macroplanning: reviewing long-term deliverables, setting weekly goals, then daily; putting it all in a calendar.

@Steve_Campbell Set up e-mail reminders so you don't miss important events. Keep things in the cloud (online) so you can access them anywhere.

@positivepresent Try Gretchen Rubin's 1-Minute Rule: if you can do it in less than a minute (i.e. put something away), do it.

NOTABLE QUOTES

*A man is rich in proportion to the number of things
which he can afford to let alone.*
—Henry David Thoreau

*A complete and accurately defined list of projects,
kept current and reviewed on at least a weekly basis, is a
master key to stress-free productivity.*
—David Allen

*Decide the outcome and the action step, put reminders
of those somewhere your brain trusts you'll see them at the
right time, and listen to your brain breathe easier.*
—David Allen

*Productivity is never an accident. It is always the result of a commit-
ment to excellence, intelligent planning, and focused effort.*
—Paul J. Meyer

*Bottom line is, if you do not use it or need it,
it's clutter, and it needs to go.*
—Charisse Ward

*I recommend you to take care of the minutes for
the hours will take care of themselves.*
—Lord Philip Dormer Stanhope, 4th Earl of Chesterfield

Time is what we want most, but what we use worst.
—William Penn

*Time equals life; therefore, waste your time and waste of your life,
or master your time and master your life.*
—Alan Lakein

Don't be fooled by the calendar. There are only as many days in the year as you make use of. One man gets only a week's value out of a year while another man gets a full year's value out of a week.
—Charles Richards

The key is in not spending time, but in investing it.
—Stephen R. Covey

If you want to make good use of your time, you've got to know what's most important and then give it all you've got.
—Lee Iacocca

*It is not enough to be busy, so are the ants.
The question is, what are we busy about?*
—Henry David Thoreau

*Until you value yourself, you will not value your time.
Until you value your time, you will not do anything with it.*
—M. Scott Peck

One worthwhile task carried to a successful conclusion is worth half-a-hundred half-finished tasks.
—Malcolm S. Forbes

To think too long about doing a thing often becomes its undoing.
—Eva Young

*You will never "find" time for anything.
If you want time, you must make it.*
—Charles Buxton

Don't say you don't have enough time. You have exactly the same number of hours per day that were given to Helen Keller, Pasteur, Michelangelo, Mother Teresa, Leonardo da Vinci, Thomas Jefferson, and Albert Einstein.
—H. Jackson Brown

RECOMMENDED READING

Getting Things Done: The Art of Stress-Free Productivity
David Allen

The 7 Habits of Highly Effective People
Stephen R. Covey

Organized for Success: Top Executives and CEOs Reveal the Organizing Principles That Helped Them Reach the Top
Stephanie Winston

Ready for Anything: 52 Productivity Principles for Work and Life
David Allen

The Power of Less: The Fine Art of Limiting Yourself to the Essential . . . in Business and in Life
Leo Babauta

Eat That Frog! 21 Great Ways to Stop Procrastinating and Get More Done in Less Time
Brian Tracy

The Now Habit: A Strategic Program for Overcoming Procrastination and Enjoying Guilt-Free Play
Neil Fiore

Lifehacker: 88 Tech Tricks to Turbocharge Your Day
Gina Trapani

Upgrade Your Life: The Lifehacker Guide to Working Smarter, Faster, Better
Gina Trapani

One Year to an Organized Life: From Your Closets to Your Finances, the Week-by-Week Guide to Getting Completely Organized for Good
Regina Leeds

6.Friends & Family

"I am defeated and know it if I meet any human being from which I find myself unable to learn anything."
—**George H. Palmer**

MOST OF US GO FROM HAVING MANY FRIENDS IN college to a scattered few nearby after graduation. No matter how successful you are in work or life, it is not half as fun without people to share it with. Your friends (and family if you're lucky) are your safety net and your support system; the ones who will pick you up when you are crumbled, bent, and broken, and the ones who will proudly celebrate your accomplishments with you, with as much pride and enthusiasm as their own.

And where would you be if it weren't for your family? Not alive, for one thing. Through the good and bad, our families shape us to become who we are as adults. No family is perfect and your parents—believe it or not—are human. It is often not until college and life afterward that we realize how hard it is to take care of one person (ourselves), let alone an entire family.

This chapter is about:

• Maintaining old friendships
• Meeting new people and making new friends
• Acknowledging the important role relationships play in our lives
• Building and maintaining strong relationships with family

JENNY'S TIPS: FRIENDS

Maintaining friendships after college takes effort.

- Make an effort to visit people after college—especially friends in new cities who may be struggling to acclimate. It will mean a lot to them.

- Give people you haven't talked to in a while the benefit of the doubt. Try not to take it personally—their absence or lack of reaching out may have nothing to do with you.

- If you are busy and feeling overwhelmed, combine social activities with other things you want to do, like exercising, eating, or running errands. Chances are those are all things your friends need to do too.

- E-mails and Facebook messages are great, but for people you really care about, a phone call is better. Aim for real-time connections whenever you can.

- If you are having trouble keeping in touch with people you care about, set up recurring lunches or dinners at a frequency that fits your schedules.

- Try to go home for the holidays if you can—it's the best way to catch up with many old friends at the same time.

- If you find yourself frequently playing phone tag with someone, schedule a call with them like you would any other meeting. It might sound ridiculous, but it works.

- Start an e-mail chain to your close friends with a bulleted list of life updates, then have them reply and do the same. My professor Lynn called this exercise "headlines" and would make a game of it by writing catchy titles for all of her updates. For example, one of mine might be: "Blake gets book published and someone other than her parents is reading it right now!"

- Schedule a weekend vacation with old friends at the same time every year—after one or two in a row, people will start blocking it off in advance, and you will all have something to look forward to.

Meeting new people takes even more work, but that is what keeps life exciting.

- It can be hard to meet people after college. Develop a game plan just like you would for finding a job or any other life goal.

- Make a list of ways to meet people in your area: volunteer, join local sports teams, or sign up for networking groups and alumni organizations. (See the exercise at the end of this chapter.)

- Friendships after college are all about cross-pollination—introduce your friends to your friends' friends (and have them do the same).

- If you have never hosted a party before, now is your chance! Social gatherings, potlucks, and organized events at your place are great ways to enrich your social life and see lots of people at the same time.

- If you live in a new area, find local spots that are busy and social (like coffee shops) to hang out in.

- Although it can be a safety net when feeling socially awkward, try not to bury yourself in your phone while waiting in line or going about your business—you will be much more approachable if you make eye contact and look interested in the people around you.

- Be inclusive of new people in your area or at your company who may be adjusting—realize they may be having a hard time meeting people and go out of your way to include them.

- Think of making friends after college as an opportunity to push yourself beyond your comfort zone: start conversations with strangers, be friendly to people you meet, and learn to enjoy the art of small talk.

- Remember that most people are just as intimidated as you are when it comes to striking up a conversation with a total stranger. Go for it remembering that the worst thing that happens is you don't hit it off. The best? You've made a new friend!

People change, and so do friendships. Sometimes you will grow together; sometimes you will grow apart. Make the best of every friendship when you can.

- Do what you can to hold on to those who matter; and realize that sometimes you have to let friendships drift.

- If someone in your life is bringing you down and honest conversations haven't helped, friend or otherwise, sometimes you just have to move on.

- Be generous with praise for your friends' accomplishments and successes.

- Be forgiving with your friends. You are not perfect either.

- When a friend is having a hard time, you don't always have to have the "right" thing to say in order to be there for them. Sometimes just letting them know you are there and quietly listening is enough.

- Don't be an energy vampire! Everyone has bad days and rough moments, but don't be the friend that is constantly complaining or dumping your problems onto other people.

- Be honest with your friends when something is bothering you. If they are truly your friend, they will listen and make an effort to respond.

- Although we are all guilty of it at times, do your best not to judge your friends for what you perceive as mistakes they are making. You may be shocked to find one day that the very things you judge them harshly for might end up as issues you have to face. Compassion, nonjudgment, and support are some of the best gifts you can give when a friend is in a tough spot.

- That said, when you see your friends engaging in dangerous or self-destructive behavior, don't be afraid to speak up. If you don't, who will? Sometimes telling someone the hard truth is the best thing you can do if you really care about him or her.

Friends are the ultimate support network.

- Our friends may not be perfect, but they really can become like a second family with nurturing and attention.

- Lean on your friends and ask for help when you need to—remember how good it feels when you get to be there for someone. Allow your friends to do the same for you.

- Make a point to uplift someone every day. Send a nice e-mail or text message and let someone in your life know you are thinking about them.

- Give compliments often (as long as they are genuine) and express appreciation for your friends. They are often the ones who rush to pick us up when we fall ... so remember to give thanks even when you're standing up straight.

JENNY'S TIPS: FAMILY

- Recognize that life as an adult takes work. Take some time to appreciate the hard work and dedication your parents put into raising you.

- Call your family often. They will appreciate knowing what you are up to.

- Forgive your parents for their mistakes. Know that they did the best they could at the time while raising you.

- Tell your family you love them. Make every interaction count. Life is short. Enjoy all the time with your family that you possibly can.

- You didn't choose your family, but you can choose to be patient and loving with them.

- Ask your parents what their biggest life lessons have been. What have they learned about work, relationships, and life?

ADVICE FROM COLLEGE GRADUATES

Friends

If you move back home from college and you don't know a lot of people, you can make friends by picking up a weekend job at some cool place. I love sports and I work at a sporting goods store and have made friends that way.
—Jason V.P., University of California, Irvine

Invest in relationships with real time, energy, and love. The large majority of people spend so much effort growing their careers and their investment portfolios that they neglect the resources that will truly support and sustain them. Our culture uses independence as a measure of success, but we have forgotten that our interdependence is what enriches our emotional lives.
—A.S., UCLA

I find the easiest way for me to keep in touch (and meet) people are at happy hours. Everyone is relaxed, excited to see each other, and just downright happy. It doesn't mean you have to go out and get wasted every week, but just showing up in a consistent manner can really go far in keeping up to date with all your friends and acquaintances.
—J.M., James Madison University

There are friends that you can't live without, and then there's everybody else. Figure out who your "people" are, both new and old, give them lots of love and support on their journeys, and enjoy it when the same is returned to you.
—Eve Ellenbogen, Binghamton University (SUNY)

Family

Your parents had a life before you came along. There MAY be some things you don't know about them. Regardless of how old you are, your parents will always remember you as the baby whose diapers they changed. So don't expect instant peer status just because you're older. Also—there is no shame in moving back in with your family. There is shame, however, in not pulling your weight around the house while you're there.
—Andrew Weitsman, University of Tulsa

Family is very important but please realize that although they have your best interest at heart, they don't know always what is best for you. Unfortunately, the people closest to you are the ones who are sometimes the least supportive. Especially if it is something they are unfamiliar with or are afraid to attempt themselves. So if you go to your family for support and don't get it, don't doubt your dream. Just find people online or in person who are going in the same direction you are going.
—ChaChanna Simpson, The College of New Rochelle

Be thankful for your family. Every family has their flaws, but they're part of what made you who you are, and you should strive to be proud of who you are. Call at least one family member EVERY day. It's easy to venture out on your own and forget the fact that your mother drove you to 10,834 practices throughout your life, or that your dad spent 85 hours teaching you how to drive when he was exhausted after work. The least you can do is call and remind them you love them.
—Ryan Stephens, Texas Lutheran/Texas A&M

Your family will be your biggest support. You are going to go through rough times: lost jobs, bad break-ups, stolen cars, and friends who come and go. Your family will always be there for you and if they are anything like mine, will shock you with how much they are willing to give. It can be very humbling leaning on your family. Just show them that you care and don't take advantage of their support.
—Jeremy Orr, University of California, Santa Cruz

EXERCISE: THE MEET MARKET

Meeting new people after college can be tricky. For each of the following categories, brainstorm a few ideas for things you like to do that might also introduce you to knew people in your area.

Sports activities/teams:

Example: Intramural co-ed softball

1. _____

2. _____

3. _____

Online activities/communities:

Example: Meetup.com or Tweetups

1. _____

2. _____

3. _____

Networking or alumni groups:

Example: Local alumni chapter events

1. _____

2. _____

3. _____

Activities that interest me (outside of home or work):

Example: Hiking, reading at coffee shops

1. _____
2. _____
3. _____

Volunteer opportunities:

Example: Working at the local food bank or homeless shelter.

1. _____
2. _____
3. _____

Groups my friends participate in that I could join:

Example: Triathlon training group on Saturday mornings

1. _____
2. _____
3. _____

Classes I'm interested in taking:

Example: Cooking class at the local community college

1. _____
2. _____
3. _____

DEEP DIVE: HOW TO CREATE A PEER SUPPORT NETWORK

Teaming up with friends can be an incredibly effective way to pursue a goal—it gives you a support system and an accountability structure that you wouldn't otherwise have on your own. Having a peer support group for a goal is more fun, and you will benefit from other people's ideas and input.

One peer support network that really worked for me was a month-long program focused on health and fitness goals that I set up with 3 other women. We created a shared "journal" on Google Docs, and a weekly tracking spreadsheet to measure how we felt (mind and body on a scale of 1–10) and whether we reached our 5 target actions (for example: running 2 times per week).

How it worked:

We had weekly Sunday calls to review our tracking spreadsheet and talk about how the week went—successes, problem areas, and what we will focus on the next week. If we had extra time, we discussed broader challenges or questions (what to do about holiday eating, for example; or how to get back on track if we screwed up). It was so amazing to have this support network—and I really have to credit it for getting my butt to the gym on lazy mornings. It gave me exactly the extra push I needed since I knew I would have to report back to my friends at the end of the week.

You can also set up a peer support network around a book (my friends and I did this with *The Four-Day Win*, by Martha Beck).

Benefits of peer support networks

- They are free!
- They provide great structure and support for pursuing your goals.
- You can get to know people through networks made of friends-of-friends.
- Support networks will hold you accountable and (hopefully) not let you give up when you fail.
- It is a great way to benefit from rich, topic-based discussions and share tips and best practices with each other.

How to create your own support network:

1. Choose a topic (not mandatory, but helpful) or central theme that you want to get support around (health/fitness, leadership, relationships).
2. Enroll some friends: give them an overview of what you want to do, then collectively decide on goals and a format for the program. Everyone should have a stake in how it works.
3. Set up the following structures:
   a) Set a start and end date.
   b) Schedule weekly or bi-weekly calls.
   c) Create shared documents to review together each week.
4. Have each person identify their goals and state what they are hoping to get out of the program or support network.
5. Hold an intro call to discuss those goals and decide on a format for future calls.
6. Start the program; adjust documents and the schedule as necessary.
7. Hold a debrief call when it ends—what worked? What didn't? What would you do differently next time?
8. Rinse and repeat (start over)—if it worked, why end a good thing?

EXERCISE: FAMILY MATTERS

"You don't choose your family.
They are God's gift to you, as you are to them."
—Desmond Tutu

Oftentimes it's not until after moving out of the house that we realize just how much work our parents put into raising us. They weren't perfect, but most did the best they could given the resources and mental energy available to them.

Take some time now to reflect on what you've learned from your family—the good and the bad—and consider what you might want to acknowledge them for when you get the opportunity.

What do you want to thank your family for?

Mom:_____

_____

Dad:_____

_____

Sibling(s):_____

_____

What do you want to forgive your family for?

Mom:_____

_____

Dad:_____

_____

Sibling(s):_____

_____

What do you want to apologize for?

Mom:_____

_____

Dad:_____

_____

Sibling(s):_____

_____

What have been the biggest life lessons that you have learned from each of your family members?

Mom:_____

_____

Dad:_____

_____

Sibling(s):_____

_____

After doing this exercise, what might you actually want to tell your family next time you see them?

Mom:_____

_____

Dad:_____

_____

Sibling(s):_____

_____

TWO CENTS FROM TWITTER

How do you keep in touch & make time for friends & family after college? Strategies for meeting new people?

@timjahn Prioritize. At the end of the day, what matters? The work you did or the laughs you had with the ones you love? Know what matters.

@MeganCassidy Be fearless. When one of your friends goes out, go with them. Be yourself. Wear something that could start a conversation (college sweatshirt, baseball hat, interesting jewelry).

@ValerieElisse If you're afraid to strike up a conversation, remember it won't be the first time you introduce yourself to someone, or the last. Go for it!

@lisaatufunwa Going alone to networking events will force you to talk and meet new people.

@rob_e_smith I made it a goal to go to networking/social events and try to meet 5 new people a month.

@pandroff Pick a weekly day/time to catch up with family & friends. For me it's Sunday afternoon.

@writeonglass Volunteer at networking events. I've met some amazing people just by checking names off of a list at the front door.

NOTABLE QUOTES

Friends

Friendship is the hardest thing in the world to explain. It's not something you learn in school. But if you haven't learned the meaning of friendship, you really haven't learned anything.
—Muhammad Ali

You can make more friends in two months by becoming interested in other people than you can in two years by trying to get other people interested in you.
—Dale Carnegie

A true friend is someone who thinks that you are a good egg even though he knows that you are slightly cracked.
—Bernard Meltzer

How people treat you is their karma; how you react is yours.
—Wayne Dyer

If you make friends with yourself you will never be alone.
—Maxwell Maltz

Friendship is born at that moment when one person says to another, "What! You too? I thought I was the only one."
—C. S. Lewis

Sometimes being a friend means mastering the art of timing. There is a time for silence. A time to let go and allow people to hurl themselves into their own destiny. And a time to prepare to pick up the pieces when it's all over.
—Gloria Naylor

Friends aren't jumper cables. You don't throw them into the trunk and pull them out for emergencies.
—Unknown

Life is partly what we make it, and partly what is made by the friends whom we choose.
—Tehyi Hsieh

Beginning today, treat everyone you meet, friend or foe, loved one or stranger, as if they were going to be dead at midnight. Extend to each person, no matter how trivial the contact, all the care and kindness and understanding and love that you can muster, and do it with no thought of any reward. Your life will never be the same again.
—Og Mandino

When you meet someone better than yourself, turn your thoughts to becoming his equal. When you meet someone not as good as you are, look within and examine your own self.
—Confucius

Be kind, for everyone you meet is fighting a hard battle.
—Plato

I am thankful for the mess to clean after a party because it means I have been surrounded by friends.
—Nancie J. Carmody

Family

No matter what you've done for yourself or for humanity,
if you can't look back on having given love and attention to
your own family, what have you really accomplished?
—Elbert Hubbard

The great gift of family life is to be intimately acquainted with people
you might never even introduce yourself to, had life not done it for you.
—Kendall Hailey

Family life is full of major and minor crises—the ups and downs of
health, success and failure in career, marriage, and divorce—and all
kinds of characters. It is tied to places and events and histories. With
all of these felt details, life etches itself into memory and personality.
It's difficult to imagine anything more nourishing to the soul.
—Thomas Moore

Family life! The United Nations is child's play compared to the tugs
and splits and need to understand and forgive in any family.
—Mary Sarton

What families have in common around the world is that they are
the place where people learn who they are and how to be that way.
—Jean Illsley Clarke

We never know the love of our parents
for us till we have become parents.
—Henry Ward Beecher

No man on his deathbed ever looked up into the eyes of his family
and friends and said, "I wish I'd spent more time at the office."
—Unknown

RECOMMENDED READING

How to Win Friends & Influence People
Dale Carnegie

The Fine Art of Small Talk: How to Start a Conversation, Keep It Going, Build Networking Skills—and Leave a Positive Impression!
Debra Fine

How to Talk to Anyone: 92 Little Tricks for Big Success in Relationships
Leil Lowndes

Never Eat Alone: And Other Secrets to Success, One Relationship at a Time
Keith Ferrazzi with Tahl Raz

Dig Your Well Before You're Thirsty: The Only Networking Book You'll Ever Need
Harvey Mackay

The Art of Friendship: 70 Simple Rules for Making Meaningful Connections
Roger Horchow and Sally Horchow

Crucial Conversations: Tools for Talking When Stakes Are High
Kerry Patterson, Joseph Grenny, Ron McMillan, and Al Switzler

What Every BODY Is Saying: An Ex-FBI Agent's Guide to Speed-Reading People
Joe Navarro with Marvin Karlins, Ph.D.

The SPEED of Trust: The One Thing That Changes Everything
Stephen M. R. Covey

Who's Got Your Back: The Breathrough Program to Build Deep, Trusting Relationships That Create Success— and Won't Let You Fail
Keith Ferrazzi

7. Dating & Relationships

"In the end these things matter most:
How well did you love? How fully did you love?
How deeply did you learn to let go?"
—Buddha

T HERE IS A WIDE SPECTRUM OF WHERE PEOPLE ARE IN terms of romantic relationships after college: you might be in a relationship with someone you met in college, dealing with a break-up due to long distance or other differences, enjoying single life before it is time to settle down, looking for a meaningful relationship that has more serious long-term potential, or maybe you are even engaged or already married.

As you learn more about yourself and what you want in life, your relationships will change and hopefully evolve, and people will come and go. This chapter will help you navigate those changes, and get clear on what is most important to you in a relationship and significant other.

This chapter is about:

- Making the most of single life
- Keeping your relationships strong while maintaining a sense of self
- Identifying what you really want from a relationship and a significant other
- Handling break-ups with grace

JENNY'S TIPS

I don't know you, but I do know this: you deserve the best.

- Make a list of your "must-haves" and "nice-to-haves" in a partner. Stick to your guns on the must-haves and don't settle. (See the exercise at the end of this chapter.)

- If you believe you deserve to be treated with utmost respect and love, you will be much more likely to receive it.

- The quality of character of people you enter relationships with is often a reflection of your own self-worth.

- If you are in a relationship that is "good enough for now" is that really good enough?

- We can learn from all of our relationships—good and bad. Where are you settling for less than you deserve and why? Where are you strong? What are you proud of?

- Don't try too hard. Be honest. The other person should like you for YOU—regardless of whatever efforts you are making.

- Life is too good to settle for someone who makes you feel less than your best.

- Pay attention to red flags. Trust your gut and follow your instincts. If something seems off, say something.

- If red flags persist, walk away. As hard as it may seem in the beginning stages of an exciting new relationship, leaving or addressing those flags will only get harder as you become more deeply involved. As Maya Angelou said, "If someone tells you who they are, believe them."

Make the most out of single life.

- Being single is a great time to develop your friendships, try new things, and generally do whatever you feel like; enjoy it!

- Be the person you are hoping to attract. Are you looking for someone happy and fit? Focus on taking care of yourself and living your best, healthiest life.

- There is a Zen saying, "Don't push the river." Let nature take its course, especially when it comes to dating and relationships. The right person will come along at the right time. In the meantime? Have fun!

- Appreciate what you already have (and are thankful for) in your life and it grows. Focus on how many great relationships and activities you already have going.

- Online dating, while not for everyone, can be a great way to meet new people in your area. Even if you don't have a romantic connection with the people you meet, it can be a way to find workout partners and make new friends.

- Even bad dates have entertainment value—chalk it up to more great stories to tell your kids one day.

- Challenge yourself to try making conversation with one new person each day. It will help you stretch outside of your comfort zone, and you never know where those relationships might lead.

- Some people are pickier than others; some will have no problem finding dates, while some will have long stretches of time with no dating activity whatsoever. Don't feel bad about where you fall on that spectrum—be patient and trust that everything will work out as it should.

When you are in a relationship, give it your best shot. Otherwise, what's the point?

- Whatever you focus your attention on becomes your reality. Remember this when it comes to relationships, and do what you can to focus on the positive.

- There are at least three parties in a relationship: you, your significant other, and the relationship. All three require love and attention.

- The greatest gift you can give someone is to listen. *Really listen.* Make eye contact, hear what they are saying, see what they are feeling. Save your thoughts and your experiences for later in the conversation—there will be plenty of time.

- Although this may be stating the obvious, it bears repeating—communication is the foundation of a strong relationship. While some conversations can be hard or scary, they're often necessary for further growth. The saying, "What doesn't kill you makes you stronger" can often apply to relationships—working through arguments or tough conversations can help improve communication and build trust.

- Instead of making assumptions (good or bad), ask questions.

- Remember that your perspective and interpretation of a situation is just that—yours. Realize that the other person is likely looking through a very different lens. Try not to get caught up in making assumptions about the other person's motivations or actions. It's easy to get worked up based on your own assumptions (our minds are great storytellers)—which is why open, honest communication is so important.

- Don't involve too many people in analyzing your relationship—while it's good to have a few close confidants, involving too many people can cloud your own feelings and judgment. Listen to your gut and focus on what feels true for you (not your friends).

- Have empathy. Put yourself in your partner's shoes as much as you can.

- Realize that oftentimes the flaws we see in others are actually the very shortcomings or fears we refuse to acknowledge in ourselves. When you find yourself being critical of the other person, ask yourself what is making you so upset; is there an aspect of their behavior that reflects an unmet need or a shortcoming in yourself?

• It is okay to want different things. That does not make either of you wrong. It just makes communicating and compromise more important. If you can't compromise, decide whether the issue is a deal-breaker or if you can just agree to disagree.

• Have fun together! Keep a running list of things you want to try: restaurants, road trips, life experiences. Take turns planning ways to check things off of your list.

The benefit (yes, I said benefit) of break-ups:

• Break-ups are opportunities to reconnect with your friends and yourself. Spend time focusing on things you enjoy.

• Recognize that change can be a good thing. Sometimes you have to walk through the fire (go through the pain of a break-up) to get what you really want and deserve.

• Although it sounds pessimistic, remember that most romantic relationships end (before marriage, and even then only 50% make it). Focus on what you can learn from your relationships and move on as best you can.

• After a break-up it is easy to idolize the other person or look back on the relationship and think that it was perfect. It wasn't, and they weren't either. If you broke up, it is probably for a good reason. It doesn't matter how things once were—relationships change and you can't hold on to how things were "back then." It will be easier to move on if you trust your gut and focus on where you are now.

• After a break-up, spend some time looking forward: what more do you want in your life? What do you want to do? Who do you want to be? What kind of relationship do you *really* want?

• You cannot truly be open to the next relationship if you are still stuck in the last one, either emotionally or physically. Realize that in order to meet that next person or be ready for your next relationship, you have to completely let go of the last one.

- If you are unable to be alone, it is that much more important.

- When going through challenging times, find activities and people that soothe your soul. Call a friend, go out to dinner, read a book, get fresh air.

- Ask for help. Have people there who will just listen and be there for you.

- Give yourself space to express your emotions—be patient and know that every feeling you have is okay. Try journaling if you are having a hard time processing everything.

- You will go through a grieving process. You will remember the sweet things and grieve at the loss. You will be angry and frustrated and have questions and may wish things were different. Remember that things are not different. Accept that you gave it your best shot and that now it is time to move on.

- Take time to rest. Switch up your routine. Or create a new routine. Listen to yourself. Your needs will change at any given moment—just be there and respond with compassion.

- Focus on gratitude—on everything else in your life that you have to be thankful for. Focus on how much you already have going for yourself. Make a list of things you are proud of, qualities that you appreciate in yourself, or people in your life who love and support you.

DEEP DIVE: STOP AUDITIONING FOR OTHER PEOPLE'S LIVES

Stop auditioning for other people's lives. Whether it's a potential job or a potential mate, make sure you aren't focusing the majority of your attention on whether YOU are good enough for THEM. Stop wearing masks and molding yourself into the person you think other people want you to be. You be you. When you are trying to make a good impression, don't forget to genuinely ask yourself—with an open mind—what value others bring to your life as well. Is the job or the relationship good enough for YOU?

Life is like Tetris: You may be a Z when the other party is looking for an I.

No one is perfect. Life is a matching process. Look for situations in which you and the other party, given that you are both imperfect, bring something to the table. Where you both add value. If it's not a match and someone tells you this or you recognize it yourself—move on. It can be incredibly hard not to take a mismatch personally—not to dwell on what is wrong with you and what you need to change or improve. Coming from a girl who loves reflection and growth, trust me—I get it. Of course there is value in being honest with yourself. But there is also value in cutting your losses and chalking it up to a TWO-WAY mismatch in which your needs would probably not have been met either.

Honesty is worth the risk.

The matching process requires honesty to be successful, which involves taking risks. It can be scary to put yourself out there and say "This is who I am. Take me or leave me, as I am." It is scary because you are putting the real you out there to be accepted or rejected by the other party (and them by you). But it's worth it—because when two parties are a fit, it works. It really, really works. And it's a wonderful feeling to be on the same page, clicking, and "in the zone" with another person, job, or team.

You deserve to be in mutually beneficial situations and relationships.

You deserve to be surrounded by people who appreciate you and light you up. You—exactly as you already are. Because life is too short to be putting on a show.

DEEP DIVE: LOW STAKES FIRST DATES

by Benjy Feen (@benjyfeen)

Picture this: you take a thousand dollars out of the bank and go to Las Vegas. You put on your finest clothes and hit the nearest casino. You buy a $1,000-chip and stride over to the roulette wheel, looking fabulous and confident. You put the thousand-dollar chip on your lucky number, and the wheel spins . . . and you spend the rest of the weekend alone in your hotel room, wondering why bad things have to happen to you.

That's how lots of first dates feel: with everything riding on the outcome of this one big chance, romance and excitement quickly give way to confusion and dejection. Sound familiar?

Don't bet everything on the first date: lower the stakes.

Low-stakes first dates: the basics

I was introduced to the idea of low-stakes first dates by—who else?—a woman with whom I was about to go on a first date. I had started meeting women through dating websites, often exchanging boastful, flirty e-mail for weeks before one of us finally felt confident enough to ask the other out.

What happened then was usually a rushed and awkward first date, and you could almost see our expectations hanging in the air like cartoon thought balloons. One day I sent off a particularly over-the-top flirtation, and got this response: "Hey, cool your jets. No need to build things up before we meet. We might not even like each other. Want to go get a beer tonight at 7?" I learned a lot about low-stakes dating on our first (and only) date.

Tip: Have the first date as soon as you know you want to have one. Don't spend six months trading witty e-mail banter. Once it's clear that this is someone you want to know better, make a date. *Flattery feels good, but it raises the stakes.* As much fun as it is to flirt, it does make it harder to keep it low-key.

Good first dates

A good first date is a shared experience of something that leaves room for casual conversation and offers opportunities to tell stories and articulate thoughts, but doesn't last too long. How about lunch?

The date needs to have a definite end: some natural and obvious point at which you two will go your separate ways. If you have dinner together, linger over dessert instead of going onward to a bar. Arrange to meet at the restaurant, rather than being picked up—and therefore dropped off—at home.

Bad first dates

Going to a party where your date won't know anyone. You'll either snub your friends, snub your date, or spend your time managing your date's experience. Or maybe all of your friends will absolutely love or totally hate your date . . . which raises the stakes.

Situations that prevent you from speaking or looking at each other. Movies and theater don't make good first dates, since sitting wordlessly in the dark for two hours is a lousy way to get to know someone.

Situations that can't gracefully be adjusted or ended once they start. A 4-hour sunset cruise is a great date . . . until you get seasick, or your date casually makes a racist remark.

Stuff you've never done that they absolutely love (or vice versa). This is a tricky one, for a few reasons. There's a good chance of awkwardness if one of you is a fish out of water. Even if you have fun, you'll be dealing with the novelty of the experience instead of, you know, being on a date. Save the fun-but-risky dates for later.

The next day: communicate clearly

You don't have to sit around waiting for the other person to call you, but do sleep on it before making that call yourself. Talk to a friend to find out how you really feel about the date.

How DO you feel about the date? What did you like? What wasn't so great? What would you want more of, and what would you want to avoid in the future? Noticing how you feel about these things will deepen your understanding of what you (a) really want, (b) gotta have, and (c) won't tolerate. That kind of self-knowledge is a key to romantic happiness.

As you reflect on these things, you may be tempted to downplay the negatives by focusing on your date's redeeming qualities, but that's not how it works: some flaws are deal-breakers, no matter what. The reverse is also true: a good date needs to have qualities you really like! An absence of huge defects should not be your standard of excellence.

If you're into it, say so. Say it simply and leave room for—ASK for!—your date's opinion on the matter. Remember, the stakes are low. If your date isn't interested in you, this is a great time to find out: leave room for that possibility while being clear about your own interest.

In the unlikely event that your date isn't interested in seeing you again: hey, no big deal. Congratulate yourself for having kept it low-key. When you're ready, make a date with one of the other several billion people out there.

If you're not into it, say so kindly and unambiguously. Don't specify a particular reason for not being into it. As a near stranger, your opinions will bear a lot of weight, so be charitable to your fellow human and just say that you didn't feel that certain romantic spark that you're looking for. Vague mild disappointment sure beats specific intense disappointment.

If you're both interested, make a second date!

DEEP DIVE: A SNAPSHOT OF
MY OWN DATING UPS AND DOWNS

The following are 3 personal snapshots on each phase of the dating process; being alone, falling in love, and breaking up. I share them with you in the hope that no matter where you are in terms of your romantic life—single or coupled, happy or unhappy, perfectly lonely or longing for intimacy—you can tap into some of the collective feelings we all share from time to time.

Single life: a note of compassion for those pesky things called FEELINGS

I often get annoyed or frustrated with myself when I'm feeling sad or lonely or anything less than jumping up and down with joy. But one night, with unwelcome no-clue-where-they-came-from-or-how-to-make-them-go-away knots in my stomach, I had a moment of compassion for myself and a major realization. I had a moment where I stopped and appreciated the fact that I *do* have feelings.

I care about people, and I care about myself. I care about living a full life. And when it comes to dating and relationships, I have a big heart. A really big heart. And I care about sharing it with someone. I have a suspicion that is called being *human*.

I am fortunate to be living a big, full, happy life. AND there is still a part of it open for a romantic relationship, just like there is always room for dessert after an incredibly satisfying meal (at least for me there is!).

Will all of my problems be solved when I meet someone? Of course not! Do I expect the next relationship to last forever? Not really—there are no guarantees in this life.

Here is what I do know: I am grateful for the 10% (plus or minus on any given day) of myself that wants to be with someone. That longs to share things like Monday Night Football and Friday night dinners.

This is where the compassion comes in. I am grateful for the part of me that can't wait to laugh with someone, to support them and encourage them, and have them do the same for me. Instead of feeling ashamed by that, or like there is something wrong with me for not intellectually rationalizing away my desire for companionship, I am going to embrace it as a strength. A strength that represents one of my core values of connecting with people. Connecting on a deep level to grow and help make each other's lives better (in a don't-worry-we're-totally-whole-to-begin-with kind of way).

I am still learning to treat myself and my feelings with respect and compassion—as I would for any friend, or any one of you. I encourage you to do the same.

Romantic life: love happens . . . if you let it

*"Love has a way of finding you if you believe in it
and have the courage to let it in."*
—Mastin Kipp, TheDailyLove.com

Romantic love is a mysterious thing. I can't even begin to generalize what the experience is like for others—nor do I dare try to give you much advice; of all the areas of my life this is one that still mystifies me.

But I can say this: one of the biggest risks I've ever taken was to let myself fall in love knowing that I could easily be heartbroken, and not knowing if I was strong enough to handle that pain.

I have always been independent, and for a long time I kept chasing achievements because I felt unlovable without them. Writing that now makes me sad—but it was true.

Letting myself fall in love meant letting someone see all of me—the good and the bad—and it meant letting go of the reins; loosening control and not trying to protect myself from pain so much. Falling in love meant lifting the oars without knowing where the river was going to take me.

I learned so much from the experience of falling in love. I learned that love is not something you do, like an item on a checklist. It is not some goal you reach, and it is not something you can dictate or control (despite my repeated attempts at being "rational").

I am sure I am regurgitating thousands of years of wisdom when I say that love is something you ALLOW. It is not a mountain you climb. It is something wonderful you sink into. They call it "falling in love" for a reason—you have to throw your hands up, let go, and free yourself of fear and insecurity in order to let love in.

When it comes to love, I've learned that there can't be conditions about feelings you are expecting in return. Love doesn't work that way because love is a gift you give to yourself and to the other person. It is the gift of allowing yourself to open up to someone without knowing how they will respond. It is the gift of letting someone be a mirror, a confidant, a friend, and lover, even though fate might take those things away someday.

Love is seeing yourself as wonderful, irresistible, and whole—and it is even better when you have the help of seeing those qualities in yourself through another person's eyes.

Falling in love is a risk. But to me, it is one of the greatest risks worth taking. I learned more about myself from falling in love and dealing with the subsequent heartbreak than I have from any book, class, or bullet on my résumé.

The break-up: a note on sadness; cloudy with a chance of sunshine

"We should bear our sorrows with greater confidence than our joys. For they are the moments when something new, something unknown, has entered into us. The more patient, quiet and open we are in our sorrowing, the more deeply and the more unhesitatingly will the new thing enter us and the better we shall deserve it."
—Rainer Maria Rilke

When I am sad, I tend to hide from the world—including my friends. I retreat into my turtle shell and won't come out until I can be happy and put-together again. I'm not endorsing this method (it gets lonely)—it just happens to be my first line of defense.

When my last relationship ended, I retreated into my "I'm fine!" turtle shell, and for many days afterward I felt like someone reached down from the sky and plucked the whole thing right off. Sadness exposed, written on my face. Tears welled up at unpredictable moments.

But I made a point to be grateful. I was happy to be sad because it represented the fact that I lived and I loved and I felt alive. I grieved that the wonderful experience was over, but to this day still feel happy for the connection and the countless moments of bliss.

While I used to shun sadness and push it aside, I learned to give it a free pass to hang out with me sometimes—to give it a voice when it was trying to be heard. As much as I may want to be happy in moments of pain, only by working through the sadness can I ever truly release it. Only by letting it in—and airing it out—can I really move forward.

There are two Rilke quotes I send to friends when they hit rough patches. In addition to the one I shared above, they are:

*"Perhaps all the dragons of our lives are princesses,
who are only waiting to see us once beautiful and brave."*

*"You must think that something is happening upon you, that life has
not forgotten you, that it holds you in its hand; it will not let you fall."*
—Rainer Maria Rilke

Sadness, vulnerability, and love are more beautiful than I ever gave them credit for. Because they are real and raw and part of living a big full life. And so is letting people in.

ADVICE FROM COLLEGE GRADUATES

Utilize the tools that are out there to meet as many people as you can until the right one comes along. Ask friends or family to set you up on dates, go to social gatherings, join a co-ed sports team, put a profile on an online dating website, participate in your community or religious activities. Your soul mate is not going to be able to find you if you just sit at home every night.
—Audrey G., University of Utah

Do your best to understand that you don't HAVE to be in a relationship to be whole. I had been in a relationship since I was 15 when I suddenly found myself single at 30. I learned more about myself when I was alone than all those years prior. It is not someone else's job to make you happy; it's YOURS. Being in a relationship where someone makes you happy is just a bonus.
—Andrea O., California State University, San Marcos

A wise woman once told me, "You have to be someONE before you can be someONE'S." This is unequivocally true. I've seen many examples of it. Be the person you want in a significant other. Be happy with yourself and your own life. You'll be a much better partner as a result and you'll also attract people with whom you're compatible. Relationships really do happen when you least expect it. It really WILL be your time, when it is the right time for you.
—Sharalyn Hartwell, Utah State University

Look at each person you date as someone who can help you learn something about yourself. Many times you might get caught up on finding "the one" and just get disappointed on every date you have. Instead, just see everything as an experience that is getting you ready for that real relationship (if that's what you want). Also, don't feel pressured to settle down; you might have other areas of your life where you find plenty of fulfillment.
—Leila Johnson, University of Denver

EXERCISE: RELATIONSHIP ESSENTIALS

We all know that no one is perfect. But a deal-breaker for you might only be an annoyance for someone else. This exercise will help you get clear on your key priorities in a partner and relationship. It may also help you get clear on whether a current or potential relationship is right for you, and illuminate ways you might also continue developing to become successful in your current and future relationships.

Significant other:

What qualities in a significant other are "must-haves"?

_____

_____

_____

_____

What qualities in a significant other are "nice-to-haves"?

_____

_____

_____

_____

What qualities in a significant other are deal-breakers?

_____

_____

_____

_____

Relationship:

What qualities in your ideal relationship are "must-haves" (for example: good communication, trust, passion)?

_____

_____

_____

_____

What qualities in your ideal relationship are "nice-to-haves"?

_____

_____

_____

_____

What qualities in your ideal relationship are deal-breakers?

_____

_____

_____

_____

Self-reflection:

It is easy to be critical of others. Take a hard look at yourself—what areas of improvement might have a big impact on your current relationship and/or your current or future partner?

_____

_____

_____

What negative or limiting beliefs do you hold about relationships that you want to let go of?

_____

_____

_____

_____

EXERCISE: RELATIONSHIP 360—PAST, PRESENT, AND FUTURE

Previous relationships:

Make a list of your most significant romantic relationships:

_____

_____

_____

What lessons did you learn from your previous relationships (the good and the bad)? How did your exes serve as teachers for you?

_____

_____

_____

What negative patterns have you followed in past relationships or in choosing significant others that you want to avoid in the future?

_____

_____

_____

Current relationship (if you are not currently in a relationship, answer these questions based on your relationship with yourself):

Where can you be more forgiving or relaxed? Where do you want to communicate or stand up for yourself more?

_____

_____

_____

What one action or change would have the greatest positive impact on your relationship?

_____

_____

_____

Future relationships:

Describe your ideal relationship: How much time do you spend together? What do you like to do? What do your friends and family do and say? How do you feel?

_____

_____

_____

What are some actions you could take to create the life and feelings you described above, regardless of whether or not you are currently in a relationship?

_____

_____

_____

EXERCISE: SINGLE OR COUPLED? CELEBRATE BOTH SIDES OF THE COIN

I'm sure you have heard the saying, "the grass is always greener on the other side"...well, that seems particularly true when it comes to dating and relationships.

No matter how happy people might be in their situations, single people sometimes find themselves coveting a good couch-cuddle or the comforts of a relationship, while those who are spoken for may find themselves starry-eyed over nights on the town, random rendezvous, and the thrill of the chase that comes from pursuing a new relationship.

Whether you are single or coupled, hopefully this exercise will help you appreciate your situation.

What are 5 things you enjoy about being single?

1. _____
2. _____
3. _____
4. _____
5. _____

What are 5 things you enjoy about being in a relationship?

1. _____
2. _____
3. _____
4. _____
5. _____

EXERCISE: PROCESSING A BREAK-UP (OR GETTING OVER AN EX)

I don't know about you, but when I go through a break-up, my head is spinning, my emotions jerk me around like a roller coaster, and I can barely think clearly enough to make it through a day at work (not to mention the fact that I may spontaneously want to celebrate and/or cry at any given moment).

If you are going through a break-up or still trying to get over someone, these questions will help you sort through your thoughts, mourn your loss, and start to see your situation more clearly. Get out a sheet of paper (or your trusty journal) and take as much room as you need to answer the questions below. Writing your answers down will make a huge difference—you may even want to keep adding to these lists as you experience new and different feelings.

What I will miss most:

- About the person
- About the relationship

What I will be thankful to leave behind:

- What I won't miss about the person
- What I won't miss about the relationship

Future relationship or partner—lessons learned:

- Must-haves
- Nice-to-haves
- Can't-stands/deal-breakers

Self-lessons learned:

• Person as a mirror: What did they teach me?

• What did I learn about myself? About relationships?

Handling the break-up (or the relationship):

• Things I'm proud of

• Things I would do differently

Feel it out:

• Thoughts or feelings I'm experiencing right now

• Feelings I may be holding back (because I might feel unjustified or ashamed) that I just need to let out

• What I'm having a hard time letting go of (about the relationship or the person)

• The vent letter (you won't send): get angry! Let out any aggression or frustration you're carrying.

Back to basics:

• Things I didn't have time for while I was in the relationship that I want to make time for now

• Things in my life that I am grateful for

Self-Love SOS:

• Activities that make me feel better when I'm down

• Ways I can take care of myself during the grieving process

• Friends and family who I can talk to when I'm feeling particularly sad

Everything happens for a reason:

- Signs or red flags that signaled it might not be the relationship I once thought it was

- Reasons the break-up is actually for the best

- Reasons I'm going to be okay

Remember that you *will* go through a grieving process after your relationship ends, even if it doesn't happen right away. You will be grieving the loss of that person, the relationship, and the future you may have envisioned for yourself. Be patient and compassionate with yourself; know that you are resilient and that you WILL get to the other side stronger, wiser, and even more ready to let great things into your life.

TWO CENTS FROM TWITTER

What is the biggest lesson you have learned from past (or present) relationships?

@cloverdew Be who you are, do what you want, work on yourself, and love will follow.

@JewelJonesPR Don't be afraid to pursue opportunities because you're in a relationship. If it's right…relationship won't hurt career and vice versa.

@thewayaliseesit Bad dates/relationships are good—you know more about what you want/don't want in a relationship.

@littlemspaige I like to relate the following advice to relationships (not strictly work): "Hire slowly, fire quickly."

@opheliaswebb If you don't put yourself out there, then you have no room to let someone in.

@positivepresent Regarding relationships, if something feels wrong, it IS wrong. Don't settle or rationalize who you love.

@irinai If there is ever a contradiction between what a person SAYS and DOES, always ignore what she or he says.

@ElleLaMode Listen to your gut. If something doesn't feel right, it probably isn't. Address it—don't let it fester…that's toxic.

@sjhalestorm Don't take relationships so seriously. You don't need to date. If you relax, it will work.

@skodai Most relationship problems have nothing to do with your partner and everything to do with your own stuff.

@ChaChanna Having standards doesn't mean you're being picky. You just know what you will and will not put up with.

@Tursita Relationships—dating, friends, family—they all teach you how to work, communicate, and succeed with different personality types.

NOTABLE QUOTES

Love is all fun and games until someone loses an eye or gets pregnant.
—Jim Cole

No one can make you feel inferior without your consent.
—Eleanor Roosevelt

What else is love but understanding and rejoicing in the fact that another person lives, acts, and experiences otherwise than we do . . ..
—Friedrich Nietzsche

To be brave is to love someone unconditionally, without expecting anything in return. To just give. That takes courage, because we don't want to fall on our faces or leave ourselves open to hurt.
—Madonna

The worst loneliness is not to be comfortable with yourself..
—Mark Twain

If you love someone, set them free. If they come back they're yours; if they don't they never were.
—Richard Bach

We've got this gift of love, but love is like a precious plant. You can't just accept it and leave it in the cupboard or just think it's going to get on by itself. You've got to keep watering it.
—John Lennon

Communication is a skill that you can learn. It's like riding a bicycle or typing. If you're willing to work at it, you can rapidly improve the quality of every part of your life.
—Brian Tracy

It takes a minute to have a crush on someone, an hour to like someone and a day to love someone—but it takes a lifetime to forget someone.
—Unknown

*The best relationships—friendship and otherwise—
tend to be those where you can say anything to the other
person but you don't say everything.*
—Audrey Beth Stein

*Never idealize others. They will never live up to your expectations.
Don't over-analyze your relationships. Stop playing games. A growing
relationship can only be nurtured by genuineness.*
—Leo F. Buscaglia

*It seems essential, in relationships and all tasks, that we concentrate
only on what is most significant and important.*
—Sören Kierkegaard

*Relationships are hard. It's like a full-time job, and we should treat it
like one. If your boyfriend or girlfriend wants to leave you, they should
give you two weeks'notice. There should be severance pay and before
they leave you, they should have to find you a temp.*
—Bob Ettinger

It is far better to be alone than to wish you were.
—Ann Landers

*People think a soul mate is your perfect fit, and that's what
everyone wants. But a true soul mate is a mirror, the person who
shows you everything that is holding you back, the person who brings
you to your own attention so you can change your life.*
—Elizabeth Gilbert

*Everything that has a beginning has an ending.
Make your peace with that and all will be well.*
—Buddha

*Don't settle because you're afraid you won't find something better.
Don't compromise because you don't want to be alone. Give your per-
fect life, lover and job time and space to grow into your life.*
—Mastin Kipp

*The aim of an argument or discussion
should not be victory, but progress.*
—Joseph Joubert

*If you are patient in one moment of anger,
you will escape a hundred days of sorrow.*
—Chinese Proverb

*The deeper that sorrow carves into your being,
the more joy you can contain.*
—Kahlil Gibran

*When we meet real tragedy in life, we can react in two ways—
either by losing hope and falling into self-destructive habits, or by
using the challenge to find our inner strength.*
—Dalai Lama XIV

*If you are waiting for anything in order to live and love
without holding back, then you suffer.*
—David Deida

RECOMMENDED READING

**Men Are from Mars, Women Are from Venus:
The Classic Guide to Understanding the Opposite Sex**
John Gray

Love and Limerence: The Experience of Being in Love
Dorothy Tennov

Difficult Conversations: How to Discuss What Matters Most
Douglas Stone, Bruce Patton, and Sheila Heen

Break-Up Emergency
Eris Huemer

Getting the Love You Want: A Guide for Couples
Harville Hendrix

**The Hard Questions: 100 Essential Questions
to Ask Before You Say "I Do"**
Susan Piver

**Why Can't You Read My Mind? Overcoming the 9 Toxic
Thought Patterns that Get in the Way of a Loving Relationship**
Jeffrey Bernstein and Susan Magee

**I Need Your Love—Is That True?: How to Stop Seeking Love,
Approval, and Appreciation and Start Finding Them Instead**
Byron Katie

8. Health

"To ensure good health: eat lightly, breathe deeply, live moderately, cultivate cheerfulness, and maintain an interest in life."
—**William Londen**

IT CAN BE EASY TO PUT EXERCISE AND GOOD EATING habits on the back burner amidst the chaos of life and work. However, there is no time like your twenties to develop good habits for the rest of your life—it will only get harder as you get older when your metabolism slows and you have more responsibility at home and work. Strong nutrition and fitness habits will give you more energy, more focus, and more confidence.

Health is an area I'm deeply passionate about. It took me a few years of on-again/off-again fitness habits to realize that exercise and healthy eating habits are really where much of my baseline happiness comes from. If I don't exercise and take care of myself, I immediately notice I feel more stressed, less creative, and often sad and robbed of energy.

Good health is a day-by-day journey (not a one-time destination), and a constant adjusting process. Through much experimentation (and scale fluctuations), I've learned the importance of portion control, healthy choices, and finding dynamic diet and exercise systems that work for me. At the end of the day, health is about doing things that make you feel happy, confident, and energized.

This chapter is about:

- Incorporating regular exercise into your life
- Identifying foods and activities you like
- Developing healthy eating habits
- Engaging peer support networks for greater accountability

JENNY'S TIPS

For optimal health, focus on the basics:

- Drink lots of water; by the time you are thirsty, you are already dehydrated. Carry a water bottle with you and refill it throughout the day.

- Find physical activities you enjoy; figure out what works for you, then come up with a schedule and commit to a regular exercise routine.

- Avoid the "all or nothing" mindset with fitness and nutrition. If you slip up by missing a workout or eating something bad for you, get right back on track. You will do much less damage than if you assume the whole day or week is shot and throw your goals out the window.

- Remember that something is better than nothing. Even if you can only exercise for 20 minutes, get moving.

- Make sure that you get enough sleep. Experiment with different amounts of sleep for a few weeks to find what works best for you—some people feel great after seven hours, some need nine or ten. It also helps your body get into a rhythm if you can go to bed and wake up at the same time every day.

- Try to focus on eating natural foods (instead of processed, prepacked food).

- Don't completely ditch your diet and exercise habits on weekends; enjoy yourself, but try to stay active.

- It is super easy to overeat when eating out: watch portion sizes at restaurants; drink lots of water, eat slowly and stop one bite before you are full.

- Try not to skip meals. Eat when you are hungry and plan snacks ahead of time if you have trouble eating healthy, filling snacks.

- • Don't get caught up in diet fads. Weight loss follows a very simple formula: you have to burn more calories than you eat in a given day or week to lose weight. That means either working out more or eating less. Neither one is a quick-fix; both will take commitment.

- Watch out for liquid calories: juice, soda, alcohol, fancy Starbucks drinks—they add up fast.

- If you use the "I'm celebrating" excuse often, realize there will always be something to celebrate. Of course you should indulge and enjoy your life, but those are the times it is probably most important for you not to go overboard.

- Do not be attached to having a "clean plate" no matter what your mom told you about finishing your dinner growing up. It's an artificial measure of satisfaction: eat until you are full, not until your plate tells you to stop. Wasting a few bites of food is better than adding inches to your waistline.

- Watch out for mindless eating (especially in front of the TV). Don't snack just because you are on the couch.

- Eating sugar will cause major spikes in your glucose and energy levels, and will leave you craving more as the day goes on. Do your best to limit sugar in your diet; it is addicting.

The Ultimate Excuse:
But I don't have time to exercise!

- You have to MAKE time for exercise. No one is going to do it for you, and if you don't carve it out and commit, something else will always come up at the last minute or take priority.

- Splurge on music purchases if it gives you the extra push and motivation you need while working out.

- Put a motivating picture on your refrigerator or pantry door so you think twice before reaching for something. Change the picture regularly (otherwise you will start looking right past it).

- Don't fall into the "I'll start tomorrow" trap, particularly with diet and exercise. Start TODAY.

- Try morning workouts. If you plan your workout at the end of the day, any number of things can interfere: you're tired, busy, still have work to do, dinner with friends, you're hungry, or you have some other social obligation. In the morning, the only thing you fight against is being tired—and you'll get over it within 15 minutes of getting out of bed. It will also give you more energy for the rest of the day. If you do work out in the morning, set your clothes out the night before.

• Hiring a personal trainer is a great way to get motivated, learn new exercises and give your fitness routine a boost with added intensity and accountability.

Tips for hiring a personal trainer on a budget:

• Ask the trainer if he or she is willing to shorten your sessions to half an hour.

• Partner with a friend and split the cost.

• Have sessions once a month or every two months, then stick to that routine between sessions until you're ready for a new set of activities.

• If personal training is still too expensive but you like the idea, partner with a friend and switch off days leading the other through a weight-lifting routine. Don't go easy on each other!

• Try signing up for group fitness classes. That will also help you vary your routine (and potentially meet new people).

Reminders to get you motivated when you get off track:

• Remember that physical health and happiness breeds confidence, which improves relationships and creates great positive energy.

• Let the bad day or week be what it is. Your body and/or mind need to relax, indulge, enjoy, and splurge from time to time. Don't dwell on it; make a point to get back on track the next day or week.

• If your slipup involved a sugar overload, make a point NOT to eat sugar the next day (so you don't fall back into old patterns/sugar habits). Sugar can be addicting (as can salt and fat; read *The End of Overeating*, by David Kessler for more on this subject).

• If you don't make it to the gym, there are plenty of quick exercises you can do in your living room while watching TV: push-ups, sit-ups, and simple stretches, for starters.

There is more to life than being on a diet.

• If you are frustrated by your diet and exercise habits (or results), try asking yourself: "What one change would make the biggest impact?" and focus solely on that for a week or two.

• Set realistic goals for your weight. Your body changes—it is likely you will never be the size you were in high school.

• It is not all about the scale—focus on how you feel when you eat well and exercise regularly. How does your body feel? How are your energy levels? Confidence? How does your clothing fit?

• Be conscious that with numerical goals (like weight or size) you risk becoming obsessed with those numbers and in many cases, you will still not be happy by the time you reach them.

Confidence is sexy!

• Be confident. Walk confidently, stand tall with your shoulders back and your head high. Attitude is everything when it comes to body image and attractiveness.

• Learn to accept the body and facial features you have. No amount of gym time or starvation can make you look like Gisele Bündchen or Matthew McConaughey if you were not born that way.

• Wear clothes and carry yourself in a way that makes you feel good about yourself. You deserve to look and feel like a million bucks—and it doesn't have to cost that much.

- If you wear clothes that make you feel good, you will probably be more motivated to work out and eat well. And the positive feedback you receive will be energizing.

- Putting time and effort into your appearance is like saying to yourself, "I'm worth it!"—which is so much more important than what you're wearing or what the scale says.

- Don't waste these early years on being insecure. You will probably look back at pictures five years from now and wish you had that body!

DEEP DIVE: 5 THINGS I LEARNED FROM ~~PANICKING~~ FINISHING A TRIATHLON

Contrary to the story I made up for many years that "I could never do a triathlon because the swimming would kill me" (not to mention my irrational fear of fish), in August of 2009 I completed the "See Jane Tri" event—a 400-meter swim, 11-mile bike ride, and 3-mile run. And lo and behold, I survived.

But there was a moment, within 30 seconds of starting, that I honestly didn't know if I was going to make it to the other side of the lake shore, let alone the finish line. I seriously considered quitting the race, even after the months of rigorous training I had put into preparing for it.

Eels in the lake were the least of my concerns.

Part of what I love about big athletic events are the months of training leading up to them. In fact, when I did the marathon in 2008, I found many of the long runs to be more enjoyable than the event itself—even the 23-miler I did alone, without any of the water stops or fanfare of race day. I appreciate the structure of a training schedule, the incremental "wins" week after week, and the commitment to completing a goal that I know will expand my beliefs about what I am mentally and physically capable of.

Where am I going with this? Given how much I love training, I was shocked when I got in the water for the first event on the day of the triathlon and panicked. Months of swim training flew right out the window, as if I hadn't even put on (or looked at) a swimsuit in the last ten years.

Seconds after the starting whistle blew, limbs started flying and I started inhaling lake water. I was immediately out of breath (mostly due to anxiety), struggling even to dog paddle. Panicked, I tried swimming the way I'd practiced, but between trying to keep my eyes on the buoy and the other swimmers (both not advisable), my head created resistance, my legs sunk too low, and my arms started doing all the work.

I couldn't relax, and I was really scared. I thought about quitting and that made me sad. *Some way, some how, I would do this.* No one said it had to be fast or pretty. So I backstroked my way around the course, calmed by focusing on the expansive, empty blue sky above, even amidst the commotion of other swimmers around me. I emerged from the water close to last. I didn't care. I smiled and ran to my bike just like the rest of them.

I reflected on the harrowing swim experience during the bike ride (glorious) and summarized my key lessons in my head during the run (exhausted):

Remember to breathe (even if every other breath leaves you chugging lake water). Sometimes the accomplishment is not speed or grace—it is literally just surviving. Finishing. Remembering to breathe.

When Plan A fails, and you're too panicked to find Plan B, trust your instincts. I hadn't done a backstroke since taking swim lessons as an eight-year-old, but nothing else was working. Did I care that I felt ridiculous swimming (in what appeared to be a casual leisurely swim from afar) on my back while everyone else powered forward on their stomachs? No. Not enough to quit.

It is all about the story you tell yourself. During a race (just as in life), there is a continual story playing in my head. It's almost like an ESPN commenter but in first person. "I am strong. I trained for this. I know what I am doing. I am panicked. I want to quit. But I am not a quitter."

The narrative goes on. In my opinion, the ONLY way to successfully finish a physically grueling event is to narrate a mental story of positivity and success.

I learned a great deal about this in the book *The Non-Runner's Marathon Trainer*, by David A. Whitsett, Forrest A. Dolgener, and Tanjala Mabon Kole. When running, there is a huge difference between saying "my legs feel like bricks" versus "I am doing fine, and this is easy." It matters. The negative thoughts will show up, but it is important to replace them with something positive. For another great book on the psychology of success, read *Maximum Achievement* by Brian Tracy.

Don't slack off on something just because it looks hard. This is a subset of the mental narrative point: don't give up on something based solely on the anticipation of hard work. So many women would approach hills during the run and start walking before they even got there. They expected it to be hard, so they gave up before even trying.

This is exactly why when I see a hill, I turn ON my burners. I run faster. Hills are mental. They are not that much harder—they just look like they will be. The same goes for life—when you see a challenge, put more heart into it. That's where it counts. You'll get to the top both ways, but feel so much better about yourself by taking the second approach.

Pay for the day. Remember how good it feels. My dad has a phrase, "pay for the day," that refers to building good exercise habits. Think of exercise like a small allowance or entrance fee that you pay for each day to ultimately live a long, healthy life. It doesn't matter what time of day you exercise, so long as you "pay" at some point (of course you get some days off—but you catch my drift).

Let me tell you something—"paying for the day" by doing a triathlon first thing on a Saturday morning feels fantastic, and the same holds true for all of the training leading up to it. Nothing boosts my happiness and self-confidence like exercise, particularly training for and completing a big event like a triathlon or marathon.

Figure out what your currency is—that vital activity that makes every day better (even if you experience resistance to start at times)—and remember how good it feels to pay for the day.

ADVICE FROM COLLEGE GRADUATES

Fitness: Don't hang it up with your graduation gown!
I did, and it was hard to get back on the wagon 15 pounds later.
—E.S., University of Michigan, Ann Arbor

Learn how to cook! Cooking is a great way to save on
your food bill and it's an easy way to feel creative. Through
my interest in cooking I have learned the value of the farmer's
market; eating local, organic, and saving money. It's also a great way
to have an inexpensive night in with roommates or friends. A good
meal and a bottle of wine split between friends comes out to just a few
dollars. The better you cook, the better you eat.
—Lauren J., University of California, Davis

Health: sign yourself up for local events. Anything! Go to
active.com and pick. It will force you to get involved and be
accountable. Life after college is busy, and you have to force
yourself to keep active. Sitting on a chair for 40-plus hours a
week is not exercise, nor is the walk to the water cooler.
—Megan S., Westmont College

Just like your credit card, don't let your weight get away from you.
Develop habits and food budgets for yourself so you don't add a pound
or two or three every year. Imagine where you would be in ten years.
—Cathy B., University of California, Berkeley

After college, I could not keep myself motivated to exercise
on a consistent basis. I've found the best way to keep committed
is to bring the team element back in. Join a recreation league,
sign up for a relay—anything that practices together regularly.
It matters less what the sport is, and more that you have people
counting on you. It takes the choice out of the matter, and forces you
to just get up (off the couch or out of the office) and exercise!
—Lauren H., Claremont McKenna College

DEEP DIVE:
MY HEALTH MANIFESTO

This is my health manifesto—a list of principles and affirmations that help remind me what is important when it comes to my own health and fitness.

- I am committed to living a healthy lifestyle.

- My body is a well-oiled machine; I keep it running as a clean system by minimizing food or drinks that are bad for me.

- I limit my intake of sugar, salt, and fat, especially foods that contain all three.

- I eat when I am hungry and I stop when I am full. I focus on eating slowly and enjoying my food.

- I find ways to alleviate stress that do not involve emotional eating (eating when sad, bored, or overwhelmed).

- I take my health/fitness one day at a time. I make the healthiest choices I can in a given setting.

- I remember the incredibly positive effects that endorphins have on my mood and confidence. Exercise is core to who I am (and to my happiness).

- I remember how confident I feel in my clothes when I'm healthy.

- I am optimistic and positive about my ability to influence and stay healthy in the future.

- Slipups and bad days happen. I correct course without dwelling on my mistakes.

- My body and I are friends, not enemies. We work together. We are a team.

- I remember to thank my body often for its health and hard work.

- I create my own destiny. I focus on today and try not to let myself worry about maintaining good habits for the rest of my life.

What is your health manifesto?

This can be a set of statements that you strive for—it doesn't have to mean you follow each one perfectly. Maintaining good health will be a lifetime work-in-progress.

- _____
- _____
- _____
- _____
- _____
- _____
- _____
- _____
- _____
- _____
- _____
- _____

EXERCISE: WIN YOUR WORKOUT BATTLES

We've all fought workout battles from time to time. You know you should exercise, but the excuses and "I just don't want to" feelings override your good intentions. This exercise will help you identify what gets in your way when it comes to working out and will help you identify habits and extra support for staying motivated.

1) What are the most common excuses you use to avoid exercising?

_____

_____

_____

2) What is more important to you than excuses like being tired or too busy (for example, feeling energized, increased confidence)?

_____

_____

_____

3) What are the key behaviors that motivate you or give you a head start on exercising (for example, setting clothes out the night before)?

_____

_____

_____

4) What times of day are most convenient for you to workout? What obstacles appear at those times that you can plan for in advance?

_____

_____

_____

5) How can you combine exercise with other things you like to do? What are your favorite ways to get moving?

_____

_____

_____

6) How will you reward yourself for sticking to your routine?

_____

_____

_____

Note: Visit my website for a handy fitness and activity tracking template.

TWO CENTS FROM TWITTER

What diet or exercise habits have helped you stay healthy after college?

@ryanstephens Just lace 'em up and get out of the door. The rest usually takes care of itself. If you eat a bad meal, make the next one better!

@Kelseyonthego It is worth it to pay for a good, close gym. Make it convenient and enjoyable. It is an investment in your future.

@cubanalaf I do yoga, swimming and kickboxing. Switch it up. You'll get bored otherwise. Make time to workout at least four days a week.

@KunbreCoach You never reach "the end" with fitness, a lesson that can be applied to all of life, really.

@solitarypanda Eat until you are 80% full. Only eat half of your plate when at restaurants. Take the other half to-go.

@PuraVidaChris When eating at restaurants, always take a doggie bag home. Great for lunch or snack in next couple of days.

@TomOKeefe1 Get the sleep you need, even if it means going to bed before 9:30. You'll thank yourself in the morning.

NOTABLE QUOTES

*It is exercise alone that supports the spirits,
and keeps the mind in vigor.*
—**Marcus Tullius Cicero**

*Physical fitness is not only one of the most
important keys to a healthy body, it is the basis of dynamic
and creative intellectual activity.*
—**John F. Kennedy**

Running is one the best solutions to a clear mind.
—**Sasha Azevedo**

*You better cut the pizza in four pieces because
I'm not hungry enough to eat six.*
—**Yogi Berra**

The pleasure of eating is not in the costly flavor but in yourself.
—**Horace**

Deprivation is the mother of failure.
—**Mireille Guiliano**

One cannot think well, love well, sleep well, if one has not dined well.
—**Virginia Woolf**

*Nothing lifts me out of a bad mood better than a hard workout. It
never fails. To me, exercise is nothing short of a miracle.*
—**Cher**

*Movement is a medicine for creating change in a
person's physical, emotional, and mental states.*
—**Carol Welch**

Tell me what you eat, I'll tell you who you are.
—Jean Anthelme Brillat-Savarin

An active mind cannot exist in an inactive body.
—General George S. Patton

Habit is habit and not to be flung out of the window
by any man, but coaxed downstairs a step at a time.
—Mark Twain

If you don't do what's best for your body,
you're the one who comes up on the short end.
—Julius Erving

Instead of giving myself reasons why I can't,
I give myself reasons why I can.
—Unknown

If you're interested, you'll do what's convenient;
if you're committed, you'll do whatever it takes.
—John Assaraf

The secret of health for both mind and body is not to
mourn for the past, not to worry about the future, nor to anticipate
troubles, but to live the present moment wisely and earnestly.
—Buddha

RECOMMENDED READING

The End of Overeating: Taking Control of the
Insatiable American Appetite
David Kessler

The Four-Day Win: End Your Diet War and
Achieve Thinner Peace
Martha Beck

Food Rules: An Eater's Manual
Michael Pollan

Get with the Program!: Getting Real About Your Weight,
Health, and Emotional Well-Being
Bob Greene

The Non-Runner's Marathon Trainer
David A. Whitsett, Forrest A. Dolgener, and Tanjala Mabon Kole

Moving Toward Balance: 8 Weeks of Yoga with Rodney Yee
Rodney Yee

French Women Don't Get Fat: The Secret of Eating for Pleasure
Mireille Guiliano

Energy Addict: 101 Physical, Mental, and Spiritual
Ways to Energize Your Life
Jon Gordon

The Absolute Beginner's Cookbook: or,
How Long Do I Cook a 3-Minute Egg?
Jackie Eddy and Eleanor Clark

Eat This, Not That! Thousands of Simple Food Swaps
That Can Save You 10, 20, 30 Pounds—or More!
David Zinczenko with Matt Goulding

The Power of Full Engagement: Managing Energy, Not Time, Is
the Key to High Performance and Personal Renewal
Jim Loehr and Tony Schwartz

9. Fun & Relaxation

"Your life is either a celebration or a chore.
The choice is yours."
—Author Unknown

FUN AND RELAXATION IS ALL ABOUT YOU—IT IS about reenergizing yourself, spending time doing things you enjoy, and creating a sense of balance in your life between work and play. When you look back at your fondest memories, most will be about good times you had with friends and family—not meeting deadlines or finishing projects at work.

This chapter is about:

- Discovering activities that make you happy
- Expanding your perspective through travel
- Finding ways to relax amidst the craziness of life and work

JENNY'S TIPS

- Everyone has an inner artist. Your outlet may be writing, drawing, painting, playing music, or dancing. Figure out what your creative outlet is, and make more room for it in your life by taking a class or setting time aside, even if it is just one hour a week.

- No matter how committed you are to your job and your relationships, if you don't take time out for yourself you won't be as effective or enjoyable to be around.

- Fun and relaxation is subjective and personal—give yourself time to do whatever it is you enjoy. Be spontaneous!

- Keep two lists: a bucket list (see the life checklist exercise at the end of this chapter) of things you want to do before you die, and a shorterterm "25 things to do before I turn 25" list (or any other benchmark that is approaching sooner).

- Figure out what energizes you. Keep a list handy for times you're feeling down or bored.

- Having fun is not just about doing big crazy things. Find fun in everyday experiences.

- If you are a planner, make a point to give yourself a completely unstructured, unplanned day every now and then. Allow yourself to decide what you want to do when you wake up, without a to-do list or set of prior commitments to follow.

Get outta Dodge!

- Set up a travel fund so you can save up for at least one big trip each year.

- If you can't afford a big trip, plan a 3-day weekend either alone or with friends. Breaking out of your everyday routine can help give you a new perspective on life.

- Sign up for airline newsletters so you can be notified when flights go on sale. If you don't want to be bothered by the e-mails until you're ready for your next trip, have them skip your inbox and go straight to a "Travel" folder you can refer back to when you're ready.

- Use travel as a way to meet new people and engage with the world around you. Even if you listen to music, make a point to talk to those seated next to you on the plane (or train)—I've made some very rewarding friendships this way.

- Take a volunteering vacation—many organizations now have volunteers contribute to the community as part of a trip (for example: teaching English for three weeks in Africa). This is a great way to learn more about a local culture, meet people, and contribute to the world while exploring it.

Life is a marathon, not a sprint. Make sure you build in plenty of rest stops.

- Make a point to find ways to refresh and recharge within each day, and especially on weekends.

- Take baths. Go for a walk. Read a good book. Do things you enjoy that allow you to slow down and enjoy your life.

- Music can be an incredibly powerful relaxation tool—as can nature. Go for a hike, a walk, a bike ride—with music, or just focusing on the sights and sounds around you.

- Spend at least 5 minutes each day in total silence.

- Before you go to sleep, lie on your back, close your eyes, and feel each limb of your body sink into your bed. Allow yourself to completely relax. Release every muscle; the tension in your jaw, in your eyebrows, in the back of your eyes, and your fingers and toes. Enjoy the feeling of total relaxation.

DEEP DIVE: MY SANDBOXED LIFE

"Is the life you're living worth the price you're paying for it?"

I tend to live my life in sandboxes. Time fenced in by limits and rules. Like the beach there is sand to play in, but like a sandbox, everything has borders; my activities often happen at preplanned, designated times.

Universe (to Me): Go to Your Room. And Don't Come Out Until You Learn to Slow Down.

I had a moment last year when I threw my hands up in the air and literally shouted, "What do you want from me Universe?! I'm listening!" On a random Wednesday after finishing a few coaching sessions, I suddenly found myself curled miserably on the floor of a conference room at work. There I was, lying on my back after almost fainting 15 minutes earlier. I felt like I was going to throw up just from sitting up to pick up the phone to cancel my next meeting. I looked almost as attractive as the eye twitch I'd been rocking that week felt.

I was feeling overworked and my body was worn-out. Because I had done nothing to change that, my body and the universe had been in cahoots to hit me over the head with physical messages until I started listening.

After reflecting on what it means to slow down (something I am not naturally prone to do), I realized that I tend to live my life in a carefully manicured, structured, sandboxed existence.

Take me to the beach!

"At the beach, life is different. A day moves not from hour to hour but leaps from mood to moment. We go with the currents, plan around the tides, follow the sun."
— **Sandy Gingras**

After the near fainting experience, I decided I wanted more room to breathe. It was time to loosen the reins a little bit; to slow down even though I didn't know how (and the thought of letting go of anything terrified me a little bit).

Since then, I've done my best to create more space in my life for ME. To just be me. And to create room for someone else to be there with me—without feeling like they are restricted to an assigned sandbox of my life.

Even though I don't always strike the right balance, when it comes to slowing down and creating space, I have committed to doing the best I can. Or not doing. I think that's the whole point.

Or as my friend Andrew Norcross said to me, "Instead of having a bunch of sandboxes, just go to the beach."

May we all find the balance that suits us best; the balance between structure and chaos; between sandboxes and beautiful beaches.

DEEP DIVE: TEMPERATURE CHECK— WHAT'S YOUR QUALITY OF LIFE?

If you stuck a "quality of life" thermometer under your tongue to get a reading on how well you are treating yourself, what would the temperature reading be? Consider your overall mood, your energy levels, your satisfaction with the set of activities you perform on any given day, and your general state of well-being.

3 Questions to take your "quality of life" temperature:

- **How healthy are my current habits?**
- **What are the areas of my life that I've let slip?**
- **What can I do to replenish my energy and feel excited and happy with my day/week?**

If any of the questions above left room for improvement, the next step toward enhancing your quality of life is commitment—choosing actions that you believe will allow you to feel healthy, happy, and energetic again. Here is a personal example:

10 small actions to improve my quality of life:

1. Exercise daily.
2. Spend time outside at least once per day.
3. Drink more water.
4. Smile when I say hi to people (including those I don't know).
5. Go to bed earlier; unplug when I get home.
6. Snooze less.
7. Engage in meaningful one-on-one conversations with people.
8. Multitask less. Focus on what I'm doing at the moment and enjoy it.
9. Take 3 deep breaths smack-dab in the middle of the day to slow me down when things get crazy.
10. Be nicer to myself.

Those are my quality of life improvements—what are yours?

10 small actions to improve your quality of life:

1. _____

2. _____

3. _____

4. _____

5. _____

6. _____

7. _____

8. _____

9. _____

10. _____

EXERCISE: CURE YOUR CASE OF "THE TOMORROWS"

"Procrastination is the bad habit of putting off until the day after tomorrow what should have been done the day before yesterday."
—Napoleon Hill

What do you make a habit out of putting off until tomorrow? What two things, if you started TODAY, would make the biggest difference in your life?

1. _____

2. _____

What is stopping you from starting today?

_____

_____

_____

How can you give yourself a boost to ensure the things you really want
to do are more likely to happen?

_____

_____

_____

Some ideas:

• Partner with a friend.

• Set a reward for yourself.

• Start small—pick one thing that would make the biggest difference and
start there.

• Don't let yourself off the hook! Push through initial feelings of resistance or "I'll do that tomorrow…"

• Write a plan the night before of exactly how you want to spend the next
day or the next weekend.

What else can you do to incorporate more of the activities you listed
above into your daily routine?

_____

_____

_____

ADVICE FROM COLLEGE GRADUATES

Have something that is just for you. Whether it's playing an instrument, running, doing yoga, reading poetry, or just sitting in your office and ignoring everyone who knocks—it's hugely important to find personal time to get away from the demands of your job, your family, and the rest of the world. When things get really tough, and trust me, they will, your ability to go to "this place" will save you just enough to get you through.
—LVL, Arizona State University

Do what is important to YOU. Even if you have responsibilities that seem to take priority, take time to indulge in what makes you joyous.
—Tara C., California State University, Sacramento

I wish I had taken more time to travel. Despite having no money, I made it to Europe for three months. If I had realized how valuable travel was, I would have figured out some sort of temporary job that would have let me make some quick cash and then travel for six months. Post-college is the best time to work out your travel bug. It's also the time in which you are most willing to put up with less than plush accommodations, so it makes it easier to save money.
—Lauren J., University of California, Davis

It's okay to be lazy. It's okay to spend a weekend on the couch watching Law & Order *reruns if that's what you want to do. Don't let it become a habit, but don't feel guilty about letting go of priorities and obligations once in a while and just vegging out. Don't let things get so hectic that you NEED a mental health weekend—take smaller breaks to prevent total burnout.*
—Jenn Bollenbacher, Tufts University

DEEP DIVE: OWN THE DAY

"The trouble with the rat race is that even if you win you're still a rat."
—Lily Tomlin

You can either choose to own the day or let the day own you. Owning the day means purposefully taking time to make the day your own before it even starts.

Not owning the day goes something like this: wake up to an obnoxious alarm clock, jump out of bed after snoozing a few times, rush to get dressed, rush to get to work, get annoyed with traffic, get bombarded with e-mails and requests and interruptions and meetings, rush to get home from work, subject yourself to bad TV, go to sleep, repeat.

Owning the day means taking some time to think about what you want to do each day. What will make you happy? What will help you start the day feeling fresh and move you through it with presence of mind?

I own my day in several ways, depending on how much time I have in the morning. On an ideal day, I spend time each morning doing the following: reading the newspaper, working out, doing at least 15 minutes of yoga, sitting down and enjoying my breakfast (either alone or with friends), having a nice cup of coffee, and listening to great music in my car on the way to work.

If it were up to me, I would do all of these every day. Actually, it is up to me. I just have to get creative and make the time for it. If you don't make it a priority to own the day and start in a way that is refreshing and invigorating, your day will run right over you, and you'll just be another rat in the rat race.

What is one thing you can do differently to "own the day" tomorrow?

_____

DEEP DIVE: HAPPINESS WITHIN REACH

"Joy is not in things, it is in us."
—Charles Wagner

What is it that truly makes you happy?

When I'm financially strapped, the first thing that comes to mind is often money. But then the question becomes "if I could do anything with that money, what would it be?" I wouldn't be happy sitting on a pile of cash if I wasn't doing the things I enjoy, so I made a list of simple, accessible things I love to do. Some cost more than others, but all can be done for less than $100, especially if you get creative!

Activities that make me happy:

1. Reading the newspaper
2. Reading a book in my favorite coffee shop
3. Going to brunch with friends
4. Going to sporting events, watching football and baseball
5. Yoga (at home or in class)
6. Talking to friends
7. Going out to a nice meal (with wine and dessert!)
8. Dancing
9. Perusing used bookstores
10. Walking my dog
11. Running, biking, or swimming outside
12. Long drives by myself
13. Listening to music
14. Traveling
15. Writing

What activities make you happy?

1. _____

2. _____

3. _____

4. _____

5. _____

6. _____

7. _____

8. _____

9. _____

10. _____

EXERCISE: MY IDEAL DAY—MAD LIB

Remember Mad Libs? Those wacky, quirky stories that required you (and friends) to fill in the blanks with whatever first came to your mind?

Mad Libs are a close cousin to the term *ad lib*, which means spontaneous improvisation. For this ideal day exercise, let yourself dream. Fill in the blanks with whatever feels most soul-stirring, not what seems reasonable, practical, or possible. It's okay if your day couldn't actually happen in real life (due to realities of travel, etc.)—the important thing is to have fun! (If you need more room, you might want to get out a separate sheet of paper.)

My ideal day

The sun is shining and after an amazing night's sleep, I stretch and open my eyes at _____ (*time*). I look around _____ (*the place I'm sleeping in*) and take a minute to appreciate _____
(*aspects of the room or environment that are appealing to you, including whether or not anyone else is there with you*).

When I'm ready to get out of bed, I put on _____ (*favorite outfit or most comfortable clothes*) and sit down to eat my favorite breakfast, _____ while overlooking _____ (*another aspect of your environment, maybe outdoors, maybe something in front of you*). I might also make time for _____ (*activity or exercise*) before or after breakfast to get me ready for the day.

After breakfast, I get really excited because I know I have the whole day ahead of me to _____ (*activity 1*), _____ (*activity 2*), and _____ (*activity 3*). What a perfect day! I might even call _____ (*person 1*) and/or _____ (*person 2*) and have them join me. And since I can spontaneously travel wherever I'd like, I will probably make a few quick jaunts to _____ (*ideal spot 1*) and _____ (*ideal spot 2*).

After a long, fun day spent doing things I love, I sit down to have my favorite meal. This is the meal I always tell people I'd choose if I were stranded on a desert island and could only eat one thing for the rest of my life. Luckily, I get to make it a fancy one, which includes _____ (*favorite appetizer 1*), _____ (*favorite appetizer 2*), _____ (*main course*), _____ (*dessert*), and my favorite drink, _____. Before dinner, I toast to a recent major accomplishment of mine that I am incredibly proud of:

_____ .

Before I wrap up for the night, I take some time to unwind (or maybe go out) with my favorite things (and/or people):

_____

_____.

I notice that I feel relaxed, happy, and joyful. I'm thankful to have

_____ and _____

in my life.

Once I'm back at home, I take a minute to appreciate what an incredible day I've had. I make a list of the reasons it was so amazing:

_____   _____

_____   _____

_____   _____

I go to sleep with a huge smile on my face. I'm proud of myself for making this day happen, and I can't wait to do it again tomorrow.

Until then,

_____

(Your Billion Dollar Signature)

Ideal day debrief:

What overarching themes made your day feel so great? What qualities of your ideal day are already present in your life? What qualities are things that you could take steps toward implementing even just in little bits? What aspects of your day might speak to longer-term goals that you want to set (financial, travel, or career)?

You may not realize that even if you can't re-create your ideal day every day or even tomorrow, you are a lot closer than you think to incorporating many of the things that made it so great. Pick one small thing you can do every day to take you one step closer to your "ideal day" vision. The small things add up!

EXERCISE: WHAT'S ON YOUR LIFE CHECKLIST?

We've all got one, whether it's actually written on a piece of paper or covered by dust in the attic of your brain. It's a life checklist—things you want to do before you die. Goals, like buying a house or reaching a certain point in your career, seem a little more serious; a life checklist is about fun, adventure, and ultimate fulfillment. My life checklist online has over 150 entries, but I have shared some of my favorites below.

Excerpts from my life checklist (in no particular order):

1. Go on a safari in Africa.
2. Write a book—*here it is!*
3. Live in New York (or abroad) for at least six months.
4. Finish a marathon (run, walk, or crawl)—*Done: October 2008.*
5. Go cross-country in an RV touring professional baseball stadiums during baseball season.
6. See the pyramids in Egypt.
7. Go river rafting through the Grand Canyon.
8. Complete yoga teacher training—*Done: October 2010.*
9. Throw a football spiral well … consistently—*in progress.*
10. Learn how to change a tire on my own.
11. Speak in front of an audience of 500+ people (not counting high school graduation).
12. Fly to a city I've never been to for a Pearl Jam concert.
13. Watch a UCLA football game from the 50-yard line at the Rose Bowl—*Done: Dad's birthday in 2009.*
14. Throw someone a surprise party.
15. Take a trapeze class.
16. Buy myself a pair of Christian Louboutin heels—*Done: June 2010.*
17. Visit every continent (remaining: Australia & Antarctica).

18. Go cageless shark diving?! (*Biggest fear...*)
19. Donate a car to charity—*Done: January 2009 (R.I.P. Gold Bullet!)*
20. Make an appearance on a major morning TV show (like *Good Morning America* or *The Today Show*) to talk about my book (*keep your fingers crossed for me!*)

Your turn! What's on your life checklist? Make sure not to censor or limit yourself to what you think is possible—brainstorm as if money or time were not issues. (*You may also want to use the online life checklist template I created at LifeAfterCollege.org/blog/templates.*)

Your life checklist:

1. _____
2. _____
3. _____
4. _____
5. _____
6. _____
7. _____
8. _____
9. _____
10. _____
11. _____
12. _____
13. _____
14. _____
15. _____

TWO CENTS FROM TWITTER

How do you make time for fun & relaxation after college? Any tips for doing both on budget?

@CornOnTheJob Being a grown-up or adult is really just being a kid with responsibilities. Don't forget to play. Every day.

@GracekBoyle There are many fun and free alternatives. Try hiking/getting outdoors, local events, happy hours & group getaways (can split hotels/cost).

@OpheliasWebb Make an hour for yourself EVERY DAY to do something you enjoy and relaxes you. Even if it's at 9 p.m. or 6 a.m.!

@ValerieElisse If you're on a budget, read or spend some time outdoors. Unplug yourself.

@Lauren_Hannah Make time for YOU every single day. Don't forget that you come before work. Do what makes you happy.

NOTABLE QUOTES

Life is not a journey to the grave with the intention of arriving safely in a pretty and well preserved body, but rather to skid in broadside, thoroughly used up, totally worn out, and loudly proclaiming—WOW—what a ride!
—Bill McKenna

Learn to laugh at your troubles and you'll never run out of things to laugh at.
—Lyn Karol

Live and work but do not forget to play, to have fun in life and really enjoy it.
—Eileen Caddy

People rarely succeed unless they have fun in what they are doing.
—Dale Carnegie

Creativity is inventing, experimenting, growing, taking risks, breaking rules, making mistakes, and having fun.
—Mary Lou Cook

Sometimes the cure for restlessness is rest.
—Colleen Wainwright

There is no need to go to India or anywhere else to find peace. You will find that deep place of silence right in your room, your garden or even your bathtub.
—Elisabeth Kübler-Ross

The quality of life is determined by its activities.
—Aristotle

If you obey all the rules, you miss all the fun.
—Katharine Hepburn

What a wonderful life I've had! I only wish I'd realized it sooner.
—Colette

Fun is good.
—Dr. Seuss

A master in the art of living draws no sharp distinction between his work and his play; his labor and his leisure; his mind and his body; his education and his recreation. He hardly knows which is which. He simply pursues his vision of excellence through whatever he is doing, and leaves others to determine whether he is working or playing. To himself, he always appears to be doing both.
—François-Auguste-René, vicomte de Chateaubriand

RECOMMENDED READING

The Book of Awesome: Snow Days, Bakery Air, Finding Money in Your Pocket, and Other Simple, Brilliant Things
Neil Pasricha

Dream It. List It. Do It! How to Live a Bigger & Bolder Life, from the Life List Experts at 43Things.com
With Lia Steakley

14,000 Things to Be Happy About
Barbara Ann Kipfer

The Wish List
Barbara Ann Kipfer

Delaying the Real World: A Twentysomething's Guide to Seeking Adventure
Colleen Kinder

1,000 Places to See Before You Die: A Traveler's Life List
Patricia Schultz

Journeys of a Lifetime: 500 of the World's Greatest Trips
National Geographic

Live Your Road Trip Dream: Travel for a Year for the Cost of Staying Home
Phil and Carol White

Make the Most of Your Time on Earth: 1,000 Ultimate Travel Experiences
Rough Guides

Raising the Bar: Integrity and Passion in Life and Business: The Story of Clif Bar & Co.
Gary Erickson with Lois Lorentzen

10. Personal Growth

*"Renew thyself completely each day; do it
again and again, and forever again."*
—Henry David Thoreau

PERSONAL GROWTH IS ABOUT TAKING THE TIME TO
figure out who you are outside of what you do or how you've
been defined by friends, family, or society; it means focusing on
who you are *being* as you go about the *doing* of your life.

Personal growth means learning about what makes you feel most happy
and fulfilled, discovering more about the core of who you are, and connecting with your life's big picture. Personal growth also means enjoying the journeys of life, not just the destinations. Just like going for a
long hike—you spend most of the time on the trail going up- and down-
hill, with just a few minutes to appreciate the view from the top. Life is a
series of challenges and opportunities punctuated by successes and
achievements; this chapter is about navigating all of that with curiosity,
an open mind, and a soft heart.

This chapter is about:

- Re-connecting with who you are at your core
- Navigating major life changes and transitions
- Turning unwanted situations into opportunities for growth
- Quieting your inner critic
- Committing to your own learning and development
- Learning how to cultivate more happiness and gratitude

JENNY'S TIPS

Live with intention.
Each day is yours to create what you want.

- You can develop as a person by default, and you can grow with intention. Set time aside to read, reflect, and write about what you want to get out of your life and what contributions you want to make.

- Spend time with people who challenge you and who inspire you to grow and be a better person.

- Personal growth is as much about relaxing and learning how to enjoy your life RIGHT NOW as it is about "doing." Realize that life will never be perfect—decide to be happy right now, in this moment.

- Do not delay your dreams. If you've got financial considerations, find a way to incorporate activities you are passionate about into your regular routine, even if just for a short amount of time each week.

Be diligent about taking care
of yourself and looking inward.

- Let yourself slow down from time to time. Focus on how you are being, not just what you are doing. If you are always on the go, you will miss precious opportunities to do this.

- Life is full of the mundane: e-mails, dry cleaning, laundry, television, tasks, and obligations. Take time to create space for your big ideas.

- Set time aside to be alone every week, if not a little bit every day. It might be hard at first, but it is good for the soul.

Change is good! Learn to love and embrace change; it is often refreshing and rewarding.

- Change often brings new opportunities into your life—new people, places, and experiences. Even if the change feels scary, fear is part of what makes life exciting; don't hide from it.

- Events that seem like failures or crises are often the biggest opportunities for personal growth. Focus on learning and on how the experience is helping you grow and evolve.

- They say everything happens for a reason. Rather than being a victim of circumstance or events, look for areas of opportunity or new beginnings. As the saying goes, "When one door closes, another one opens."

- Uncertainty often breeds fear, and fear can be paralyzing. Don't let that happen to you! Consider what is in your power to change, and try not to worry too much about the rest.

Conduct periodic values tune-ups to re-connect with what is most important to you.

- Personal growth is about checking-in with your values from time to time to ensure that you are living in alignment with your true self. *(Refer back to Chapter 1 for the values exercise.)*

- If you're not living according to your key values, you'll likely be tense and sad. At times like these, look inward: what contracts are you breaking with yourself? How are you letting yourself down?

- There is a lot of information out there in the personal growth genre that can help guide you on your journey to learning more about yourself. Figure out what format works for you (blogs, podcasts, books, audiobooks, getting a life coach, etc.) and explore.

- Remember that you are not your past, your emotions, your relationships, or your job. You are the person underneath that.

Be kind and compassionate with yourself.

- Where you are now is perfect. It will help you get wherever you are going tomorrow.

- We've all got an inner critic that tells us we are not good enough in some way. Learn to notice the difference between subjective opinions from your inner critic and actual facts. (See the "Inner-critic Inventory"exercise at the end of this chapter.)

- Managing your inner critic is not about making the voice go away completely—it won't. It is about turning down the volume—or changing the channel. Are you tuned into inner-critic radio all day? When you notice, consciously shift gears to something more encouraging (this takes practice).

Be thankful. Give yourself credit for how far you have already come, and realize how abundant your life already is.

- Gratitude is important—take time every day to appreciate the simple things in your life that you are thankful for, like your health and your family.

- Having a bad day? Stop and mentally list five things you are thankful for. You might also consider keeping a gratitude journal and writing five things in it every day.

- Getting involved in the community through volunteer work is another great way to get perspective on your life. Helping those less fortunate than you will remind you of everything that you have to be thankful for. Depending on the nature of the work, it might also be a great résumé builder (not to mention that it's good karma!).

- Write thank-you notes when you are feeling down; you will uplift others and likely generate some warm-fuzzy feelings for yourself too.

DEEP DIVE:
THE PARABLE OF THE TRAPEZE

This is one of my favorite stories about change. It's an excerpt from Danaan Parry's book, Warriors of the Heart, *and is printed with permission from the Earthstewards Network.*

Turning the Fear of Transformation into the Transformation of Fear

by Danaan Parry

Sometimes I feel that my life is a series of trapeze swings. I'm either hanging on to a trapeze bar swinging along or, for a few moments in my life, I'm hurtling across space in between trapeze bars.

Most of the time, I spend my life hanging on for dear life to my trapeze-bar-of-the-moment. It carries me along at a certain steady rate of swing and I have the feeling that I'm in control of my life.

I know most of the right questions and even some of the answers.

But every once in a while as I'm merrily (or even not-so-merrily) swinging along, I look out ahead of me into the distance and what do I see? I see another trapeze bar swinging toward me. It's empty and I know, in that place in me that knows, that this new trapeze bar has my name on it. It is my next step, my growth, my aliveness coming to get me. In my heart of hearts I know that, for me to grow, I must release my grip on this present, well-known bar and move to the new one.

Each time it happens to me I hope (no, I pray) that I won't have to let go of my old bar completely before I grab the new one. But in my knowing place, I know that I must totally release my grasp on my old bar and, for some moment in time, I must hurtle across space before I can grab onto the new bar.

Each time, I am filled with terror. It doesn't matter that in all my previous hurtles across the void of unknowing I have always made it. I am each time afraid that I will miss, that I will be crushed on unseen rocks in the bottomless chasm between bars. I do it anyway. Perhaps this is the essence of what the mystics call the faith experience. No guarantees, no net, no insurance policy, but you do it anyway because somehow to keep hanging on to that old bar is no longer on the list of alternatives. So, for an eternity that can last a microsecond or a thousand lifetimes, I soar across the dark void of "the past is gone, the future is not yet here."

It's called "transition." I have come to believe that this transition is the only place that real change occurs. I mean real change, not the pseudo-change that only lasts until the next time my old buttons get punched.I have noticed that, in our culture, this transition zone is looked upon as a "no-thing," a noplace between places. Sure, the old trapeze bar was real, and that new one coming towards me, I hope that's real, too. But the void in between? Is that just a scary, confusing, disorienting nowhere that must be gotten through as fast and as unconsciously as possible?

NO! What a wasted opportunity that would be. I have a sneaking suspicion that the transition zone is the only real thing and the bars are illusions we dream up to avoid the void where the real change, the real growth, occurs for us. Whether or not my hunch is true, it remains that the transition zones in our lives are incredibly rich places. They should be honored, even savored. Yes, with all the pain and fear and feelings of being out of control that can (but not necessarily) accompany transitions, they are still the most alive, most growth-filled, passionate, expansive moments in our lives.

We cannot discover new oceans unless we have the
courage to lose sight of the shore.
—Anonymous

So, transformation of fear may have nothing to do with making fear go away, but rather with giving ourselves permission to "hang out" in the transition between trapezes. Transforming our need to grab that new bar, any bar, is allowing ourselves to dwell in the only place where change really happens. It can be terrifying. It can also be enlightening in the true sense of the word. Hurtling through the void, we just may learn how to fly.

DEEP DIVE:
THE COMPLEXITY OF CHANGE AND
THE BEAUTY IN EMBRACING IT

*"Uncertainty is the only certainty there is, and knowing
how to live with insecurity is the only security."*
—John Allen Paulos

At its best, change inspires feelings of possibility, exhilaration, new beginnings, and opportunity. Making a change can be a breath of fresh air, a moment of pride, a powerful personal statement about what you stand for.

But change can also produce a great deal of fear, anxiety, confusion, and sadness. Anyone who has experienced a difficult break-up probably knows what I'm talking about—the yo-yo between feelings of freedom and feelings of dread. Sadness over the loss, wrestling with unanswerable questions about why it happened, and uncertainty about what the future will hold. Sure—there may also be relief, excitement, and hope—but it would be a mistake not to acknowledge the full spectrum of feelings.

Sometimes you choose to change; you make a hard decision, quit your job, end your relationship, or move to another city. Sometimes you waffle about making changes—you weigh pros and cons without ever reaching a decision or taking action. Sometimes you want a situation to change but don't quite know how to make it happen.

And sometimes change chooses you whether you are ready for it or not. You get fired, get dumped, lose a loved one. These are not the changes that feel immediately exhilarating and hopeful. But in time, these are often the changes we learn the most from. The changes that make us who we are and push us to question our assumptions about the way life works. These are the changes that encourage us to stop for a moment and reevaluate our priorities and the direction we want our lives to take.

Enjoy the unknown and the suspense of not knowing exactly what is next. Be patient with yourself, and be patient with your friends. Realize that change is complex and that we all have different thresholds for it. When we are ready and when it really counts, we all have the power within us to make and embrace big changes.

DEEP DIVE: EMPTY SPACES (AND MOVING PAST LONELINESS)

"Periods of recovery are likewise intrinsic to creativity and to intimate connection. Sounds become music in the spaces between notes, just as words are created by the spaces between letters. It is in the spaces between that love, friendship, depth and dimension are nurtured."
—**Jim Loehr**

As I mentioned earlier, I live a life that I am incredibly grateful for; a life full of activities, work, people, and fun. And yet, particularly at times of transition, I can feel overcome by emptiness. Empty spaces that are at first unwelcome, but ultimately absolutely necessary.

How my empty spaces show up

One day last year, a few weeks after a break-up, a familiar feeling started sweeping over me as I dropped my friend off after coffee. I got a lump in my throat, a sense of dread, as I drove back to my empty house, where there was no one waiting for me.

I love my condo—it is one of my proudest financial achievements. I live alone and on most days, I am incredibly thankful for my solitude and personal space. But as I drove home that day with no plans for Saturday night (intentional because I had been sick), a feeling of total emptiness consumed me. I felt taunted by the running to-do list in my mind, of all the projects I could be working on but didn't want to start.

My eyes welled up with tears and voices started sneering in the back of my mind. "See? You can't be alone. You say you're happy by yourself but you're not. This is proof." I knew that voice was wrong, but it still stung.

I know now that in those moments of near panic, if I can just get past them, there are deeper truths waiting. There are several lessons I learned as a result of pushing through those empty spaces:

1. Physical messages:
When your body talks, listen.

There was a period of work last year where I got sick 4 times in 4 months—more than I'd been sick in the last 4 years COMBINED. I was extremely fatigued—no amount of sleep seemed to be enough. It also happened to coincide with a time in which I was experiencing a lot of relationship ups and downs. I should have seen my deteriorating health coming from a mile away. If I had been paying closer attention, I would have seen that I'd been running myself into the ground and ignoring deeper feelings that needed to be dealt with.

On more than one occasion, I had to stop in the stairwell at work and just breathe. In those moments, my eyes would grow wide and I would get struck with the sudden urge to drop every single project, task, and friend I had committed anything to. To completely cancel my schedule, my projects, and my to-do lists because it was all too overwhelming. I didn't run away or let anything fall apart, but I realized I simply couldn't continue to operate at a pace that made me feel that way on a regular basis.

I believe our physical health is a reflection of our mental and emotional states of mind. Our bodies are smart. They know what we need. My body demanded that I bring my crazy life to a screeching halt and readjust. Get my emotional ducks in a row. Reprioritize and give myself permission to take a time-out. And in those time-outs, I allowed myself to sink into the empty spaces of my life. The spaces that were not filled with activities or people—just me. I tended to avoid them because they felt lonely—very lonely—at first.

2. Break-ups: Empty on overdrive

When I slow down, particularly after a break-up and when the weekend comes, I notice empty spaces in the day that weren't there before. Where I was once laughing and smiling, replaying a fun conversation or looking forward to a future one, there is suddenly nothing. Nothing but quiet.

In an effort to avoid the emptiness, I might make phone calls or refresh my e-mail inbox, Twitter stream, and feed reader. I seek distractions to shove in the empty spaces that I know I am avoiding. But deep down, I know that none of those things are going to bring back the giddy excitement that I was so used to.

I know that the only way out is through—to be quiet, and to let the emptiness exist. To be patient with myself and pay attention to what I truly want and need. And to suffer through the empty spaces instead of stuffing them with temporary relief instead.

3.Big goals: The bigger the project, the bigger the spaces.

Writing a book is one of the projects that I feel I was born to do in my lifetime. But the writing process was a roller coaster for me—I experienced a lot of tension between having the end in mind, but getting overwhelmed and overcome with doubt at several points throughout the process.

During the workweek I fantasized about working on my book during weekends; spending time alone in coffee shops or in front of my fireplace, writing. *Oooooh, aahhhh. So romantic.* But when the time would come to sit down and get to work, I would get blindsided and intimidated by the emptiness. I became acutely aware that I was working on this project alone. That at the end of the day, its success depended on me—on my ideas and my commitment (with help from family and friends, of course). I eventually learned how to push through those empty spaces and even approach the challenge of my work with excitement, but it wasn't easy at first. (*The War of Art* by Steven Pressfield really helped me with this.)

Walk through the fire; life ~~will just~~ might throw a party for you on the other side.

What do red flags, break-ups, and big goals have in common? Empty spaces materialize when activities stop. They happen when a relationship ends, and when a big, important project is on the horizon or just completed. Empty spaces can be scary, lonely, and sad at first. They can feel paralyzing. But when the empty spaces show up—if we let them—that is exactly when our lives get quiet enough to listen for what is next.

So make the hard choices. Stride boldly through the fire. Sit with your empty spaces and see what happens.

ADVICE FROM COLLEGE GRADUATES

Thoughts create our reality—they are the billion grains of pollen, one of which generates a 300-foot redwood tree. If you think negative thoughts, your tree will be weak. All emotional pain can be transformed into artistic expression—this is why art exists. Go back to early or current trauma and write / dance / paint / sing it out of your soul—clean house!
—Jim B., Harvard University

I've learned to allow myself to be sad. I've always been a very positive person, but I've had moments where I just wanted to let go and let everything out, and I did. It felt liberating, and made me feel even more grateful for everything that I have.
—Megan Cassidy, Syracuse University

When everything is in chaos, there's always one thing you can control: yourself. Take a break, relax for a minute, and think things through. Just because everything else is going crazy doesn't mean you have to as well. A lot of the situations where you're in crisis mode, panic, stress, or anger end up turning into stories you share with friends. Funny how that works.
—Andrew Weitsman, University of Tulsa

Whenever my inner critic decides to give her input, I respond with, "Isn't that interesting? I wonder why you think that?" It sounds silly, but it's a little change in thought that takes the judgment voice out of it. You can't grow when you're too busy judging yourself and feeling guilty about things you can't change. Taking the judgment out lets you look objectively at the situation and you may find that what you normally berate yourself for is actually an ingenious new way of doing something.
—Andi Norris, Chapman University

DEEP DIVE: MAKING THE SHIFT
FROM RESISTANCE TO GRATITUDE

This is about appreciating the less obvious gifts in my life—things I may resist at first, but that are truly where some of my biggest lessons come from. In addition to appreciating our blessings, I believe it is important to take a step back and appreciate the blessings-in-disguise too.

I appreciate the days I work so hard I can barely remember to eat lunch because I feel important, and I enjoy my vacation days that much more.

I am thankful for the chance to lead big, (at times) intimidating projects at work, because it means someone believes in me and because those projects push me to grow in ways I couldn't plan for or predict.

I appreciate my overflowing inbox because it means my life and work are abundant, and that people care.

I was secretly happy when my car broke down because it gave me the kick I needed to bike to work and enjoy fresh, cold air every morning.

I am thankful for the 6-month writer's block that I experienced while working on this book because it helped me reconnect with myself, my message, and my work.

I am grateful for the low moments in my life; the moments of despair, sadness, and disappointment because they enable me to be more compassionate as a listener, coach, and friend.

I am thankful for all the time that I've been single because I've filled my time with incredibly enriching people and projects.

I appreciate my imperfections because perfection is boring.

I am thankful that I don't have everything figured out, because where is the fun in that?

Your Turn: What blessings-in-disguise, failures, or mistakes are you grateful for?

Work:

_____

_____

Money:

_____

_____

Home:

_____

_____

Friends:

_____

_____

Family:

_____

_____

Dating & Relationships:

_____

_____

Other:

_____

_____

EXERCISE: THE GRATITUDE LIST

When life doesn't seem to be going our way, it can be easy to lose perspective and feel like the sky is crashing down on us. Our vision becomes clouded and we lose our perspective on how much we truly have to be thankful for.

If you can, take a few minutes every day to list or give thanks for all of the blessings in your life. This can be a particularly powerful exercise when you are having a bad day, but you might even consider keeping a gratitude journal on a regular basis, no matter what is going on in your life.

I'll kick the exercise off with 10 things I am grateful for:

My health, my family's health, my job, my house, my car, my ability to exercise, my access to great food, the loving support of my friends, family, and blog readers, travel opportunities, and my dog Patches.

What is on your gratitude list?

1. _____
2. _____
3. _____
4. _____
5. _____
6. _____
7. _____
8. _____
9. _____
10. _____

EXERCISE: CREATE YOUR "WHY I'M GREAT" FILE

Sometimes life just does not go the way you want it to. You didn't get the job you wanted, you had a bad day at work, you put your foot in your mouth, or you made a huge mistake. It's during times like these when you might need a pick-me-up—a reminder of all the great things you've done in your life to keep you going.

Take a few minutes to add top accomplishments, proudest moments, and best qualities to your "why I'm great" file—it may come in handy sometime (or at the very least, bring a smile to your face).

Top 10 accomplishments (from childhood to now):

1. _____

2. _____

3. _____

4. _____

5. _____

6. _____

7. _____

8. _____

9. _____

10. _____

Proudest moments:

Describe in more detail 3 of your proudest moments: How did you feel? How did others respond? What happened leading up to those moments?

1. _____

   _____

   _____

2. _____

   _____

   _____

3. _____

   _____

   _____

Best qualities:

Make a list of your best qualities (no inner critic allowed!). What do you love about yourself? What makes you great? List physical and personality traits.

1. _____
2. _____
3. _____
4. _____
5. _____
6. _____
7. _____
8. _____

9. _____

10. _____

11. _____

12. _____

13. _____

14. _____

15. _____

DEEP DIVE: ENOUGH

If I gave you a dollar for every time you thought yourself not good enough in some way, how much money would you have earned last week? Last year? In your lifetime? There are generally three kinds of "enoughs." Materialistic—money, things, possessions; relationships—friends, family, significant other; and personal—success, looks, smarts, time, etc.

What seems a common thread is the nagging thoughts that we all experience around the concept of "enough." If you are constantly longing for the past or waiting for the future, your entire life will be spent—well, longing or waiting. Joy is fleeting if we don't stop to appreciate where we are now, and remember that who we are and where we are is enough.

So instead of waiting for the future—for some future state where you suddenly have enough or are enough, be the future. Live and embody it; act as though it were here. It is.

There is no there, or better state. Make the most of this one—it is right where you should be—and the only place that is real.

You already have everything you need.

You may have heard the saying, "It's not what you've got, it's what you do with it." Well, what if I told you that you already have all of the skills, resources, and talent you need to pursue what you really want? What if you already knew all the right people? What if your current job or situation was the perfect one to equip you with the lessons you need for your future goals and dreams? What if your next opportunity was already available to you?

Let's try it this way: You already have all of the skills, resources, and talent you need. Do you want to change jobs? Start a blog? Write, dance, exercise, sing, or play more? You probably have all the skills you need already. So face those obstacles and fears head-on and MAKE room for what you really care about in your life. Know that it won't always be easy, nor is it supposed to be. Sometimes we have to hit major dips before we can move forward. Get out there anyway. Step fully into what you want and crush it.

EXERCISE: INNER-CRITIC INVENTORY

For this exercise, I want you to summon your inner critic. The voice you're always trying to get rid of when you're getting ready to do big things. There are some surefire ways to bring your inner critic to the party: think of a big goal, a big change you want to make, or make a list of what makes you unique and lovable.

Your inner critic is the voice in your head that tells you what's wrong with you and why you or your ideas will fail. Your inner critic wants to protect the status quo, and the best way to do that is by discouraging you from change.

For each question, I'll share some of my own inner-critic voices because it might help you remember ones of your own. Even just typing these messages makes me angry (and a little sad) because I know they're not true—but it's important to me that I share them with you so you know that you're not alone in whatever inner-critic messages you hear.

Another way to do this exercise is by keeping a sheet of paper handy when you're reading this book, working on goal-setting or going about your day. When an inner-critic message pops into your head, just notice it and write it down—add it to the inventory.

What are some of the messages your inner critic tells you?

Some of mine: you aren't lovable, you aren't skinny/pretty/etc. enough, you are too young to be credible in the career you want, but at the same time you're too old for it. Oh—and you'll never be truly happy. You're just not built for it. Except when you ARE happy, you should remember that it will all probably come crashing down at any minute.

- _____

- _____

- _____

- _____

- _____

In what ways has your inner critic been helpful or gotten you this far? What is the price you pay?

My inner critic tries to be helpful by making me a perfectionist, very achievement-oriented, and hyper-focused on trying to be good at everything. It has helped in the sense that I am independent, driven, and committed to my goals, and it has pushed me to develop my skills and successes in many areas of my life.

The cost is that I feel like I'm never enough—and it is exhausting.

When I am constantly striving for the next big thing and trying to be "perfect" to please my inner critic, I don't actually get to just be myself. Self-love becomes conditional on external measures.

_____

_____

_____

_____

_____

_____

_____

_____

If you could personify your inner critic, what would she or he look like? What type of figures or professions best represent your inner critics? (You might have more than one.)

Some of mine: a court jester that points and laughs at me whenever I feel sad or lonely; a drill sergeant that yells at me to work out more/harder who wants to be sure I keep every extra pound off in order to be lovable; a member of the "fashion elite" who looks down her nose at me and never thinks I look stylish or pretty enough; and a schoolteacher who has her red pen ready, itching to give me an "F" as soon as I mess up or don't reach her ridiculously high success metrics.

- _____

- _____

- _____

- _____

- _____

What are some mantras that your inner critic preaches?

Some of mine: if you fail you DIE; if you can't do something perfectly the first time (overnight, with no time to practice or make mistakes) you might as well not try; feeling sad is your own fault—it's clearly because YOU are doing something wrong—you failure!

- _____
- _____
- _____
- _____
- _____

What do you know in your gut to be more true than those inner-critic messages?

For me: I know that I am lovable outside of the way I look or the things I accomplish. In fact, people love me more when I share my flaws and vulnerabilities. Nobody is perfect. I know that there is great valor and fulfillment in taking risks and trying new things, even if I am not successful by popular measures. I also know that every time I try something, I fumble my way through and eventually come out successful and confident.

I know that I always feel better when I'm taking action, not just letting my inner critic hold me back. I know that those inner-critic voices don't define me, and in fact—when they show up it means that I'm exactly on the right track. They wouldn't be there if I were not tackling big things or making big changes.

_____
_____
_____
_____

_____

_____

_____

The goal of this exercise is not to eliminate inner-critic messages completely as that would surely be a futile task, but rather to start noticing them for what they are and replacing them with more positive thoughts instead.

The goal is for you to recognize when you are tuned into "inner-critic radio" and turn down the volume (say from 8 to 2) or change the channel entirely. When you start to notice your inner-critic messages as you go about your day, practice replacing them with what you know in your gut to be more true. This is like building a muscle—it takes practice, and you *will* get better at it over time.

Finally, don't beat yourself up for having inner critics in the first place—we all do. Are you smart, tenacious, and creative? Well, your inner critic probably is too … which makes it that much more important to start calling it out!

Some ways to dismiss and defuse your inner critic:

• Add to your inner-critic inventory when you notice the voices.

• Rate yourself on a scale of 1–10 every day for two weeks based on how well you noticed and quieted your inner-critic voices.

• Keep a journal and notice how you feel about yourself on any given day.

• Do a journal exercise that I like to call "The Committee": if you are the CEO of You, Inc., who are all of the board members at the table during your decision-making meetings? What are their personalities and behaviors like? What are each of their priorities? What about their body language? Who speaks more loudly than others? Who gets ignored that wants to be heard?

My committee members include the personal trainer; the little girl (who looooves dessert and cupcakes); the Zen-like yoga teacher; the obnoxiously stubborn hard-driving executive woman (wearing a black power suit and five-inch heels); and the free-spirit hippie-chick who just wants me to chill out and love everyone and everything.

• Make up a counterargument or message that you can say to your inner critic. Mine is "That is one opinion," then I quickly think up something that feels more true for me (like "But that is just not true. I can do this" or "I deserve to be happy, etc.").

TWO CENTS FROM TWITTER

What has been your biggest blessing-in-disguise life experience since graduating from college?

@**Dmbosstone** Biggest blessing: failing at work for the first time ever. Learn to fail and you won't be afraid to take risks.

@**ChaChanna** Not getting a job and having to freelance, which led me to be brave enough to start my own business.

@**TomOKeefe1** Following my gut, and doing a year of service. It's "ruined" me for life, in a good way.

@**sjhalestorm** Not having any professional plans set immediately after college turned out incredible. Met TONS of great people and friends by networking.

NOTABLE QUOTES

*Live with intention. Walk to the edge. Listen hard.
Practice wellness. Play with abandon. Laugh. Choose
with no regret. Appreciate your friends. Continue to learn.
Do what you love. Live as if this is all there is.*
—Mary Anne Radmacher

*Those people who develop the ability to continuously
acquire new and better forms of knowledge that they
can apply to their work and to their lives will be the movers
and shakers in our society for the indefinite future.*
—Brian Tracy

*The jump is so frightening between where I am and where I want to
be . . . because of all I may become I will close my eyes and leap!*
—Mary Anne Radmacher

*The key to motivation is motive. It's the why. It's the deeper "yes!"
burning inside that makes it easier to say no to the less important.*
—Stephen R. Covey

*Life is brief, even at its longest. Whatever you
are going to do with your life, get at it.*
—Jim Rohn

*Follow effective action with quiet reflection.
From the quiet reflection will come even more effective action.*
—Peter Drucker

*None of us will ever accomplish anything excellent or commanding
except when he listens to this whisper which is heard by him alone.*
—Ralph Waldo Emerson

Each player must accept the cards life deals him or her:
but once they are in hand, he or she alone must decide
how to play the cards in order to win the game.
—Voltaire

Your worst enemy cannot harm you
As much as your own thoughts, unguarded.
But once mastered, No one can help you as much.
—The Dhammapada

If you follow your bliss, you put yourself on a kind of track,
which has been there all the while waiting for you, and the life that
you ought to be living is the one you are living.
—Joseph Campbell

To be nobody but yourself—in a world which is doing its best, night
and day, to make you everybody else—means to fight the hardest bat-
tle which any human being can fight; and never stop fighting.
—E. E. Cummings

People are always blaming their circumstances for what they
are. I don't believe in circumstances. The people who get on in
this world are the people who get up and look for the circumstances
they want, and, if they can't find them, make them.
—George Bernard Shaw

You cannot jump across the Grand Canyon in two small leaps.
—Anonymous

Every desire you have at its core exists because you think
attaining it will make you happy; but happiness can only be attained
in the present moment. Therefore any desire you have to be happy in
the future is blocking your ability to be happy now. Only when you are
at peace with what is now, will you ever find happiness now.
—Mastin Kipp

I will waste not even a precious second today in anger or hate or jealousy or selfishness. I know that the seeds I sow I will harvest, because every action, good or bad, is always followed by an equal reaction. I will plant only good seeds this day.
—Og Mandino

Our deepest fears are like dragons guarding our deepest treasures.
—Rainer Maria Rilke

If your compassion does not include yourself, it is incomplete.
—Buddha

Most people believe the mind to be a mirror, more or less accurately reflecting the world around them, not realizing on the contrary that the mind itself is the principal element of creation.
—Rabindranath Tagore

To live only for some future goal is shallow. It's the sides of the mountain that sustain life, not the top.
—Robert M. Pirsig

I have just three things to teach: simplicity, patience, compassion. These things are your greatest treasures.
—Lao-tzu

When you feel that you have reached the end and that you cannot go one step further, when life seems to be drained of all purpose; what a wonderful opportunity to start all over again, to turn over a new page.
—Eileen Caddy

RECOMMENDED READING

The Big Leap: Conquer Your Hidden Fear
and Take Life to the Next Level
Gay Hendricks

Living With Joy: Keys to Personal Power &
Spiritual Transformation
Sanaya Roman

Taming Your Gremlin: A Surprisingly Simple Method
for Getting Out of Your Own Way
Rick Carson

Wherever You Go, There You Are: Mindfulness Meditation in
Everyday Life
Jon Kabat-Zinn

The Power of NOW: A Guide to Spiritual Enlightenment
Eckhart Tolle

Welcome to Your Crisis: How to Use the Power of
Crisis to Create the Life You Want
Laura Day

Self-Meditation: 3,299 Mantras, Tips, Quotes, and Koans for
Peace and Serenity
Barbara Ann Kipfer

The Four Agreements: A Practical Guide to Personal Freedom
Don Miguel Ruiz

The Wisdom of the Enneagram: The Complete Guide to Psy-
chological and Spiritual Growth for the Nine Personality Types
Don Richard Riso and Russ Hudson

The War of Art: Break Through the Blocks and
Win Your Inner Creative Battles
Steven Pressfield

11. Closing Thoughts

*"Progress always involves risk; you can't
steal second base and keep your foot on first."*
—Frederick Wilcox

I WANT TO CLOSE WITH A LITTLE STORY ABOUT HOW THIS book came to be. The arc of this story has applied to every major achievement in my life, which goes beyond financial and career successes. This is a story of vision followed by inner critics. A story of goals so big I was afraid to say them out loud; of self-doubt and self-defeat but also one of incredible support and serendipity. This is a story of how one baby step at a time—one tentative foot in front of the other—can lead to great things.

Surviving Self-Doubt

Ever since I was a little girl, I dreamed of being an author. I buried myself in a new book every week. I catalogued the books in my bedroom like a library and gave late slips out to people who didn't return them on time. I ran a monthly family newspaper operation out of my living room for ten years, and I went on to become the editor in chief of my high school newspaper and the California High School Journalist of the Year.

But when it came time to write this book, I felt flooded with doubt and worry, as though someone dunked my head under a rushing faucet of inner-critic voices. *"The book has already been written; I'm not smart enough, I'm not interesting enough; I'm too old, I'm too young; nothing tragic has ever happened to me, I'm not special, I've never lived abroad or had crazy life experiences to talk about; I'm not sensational or funny enough, and I'm not good at sales and marketing."* Are you exhausted? I am exhausted just thinking about dealing with all that emotional garbage!

After I wrote the first draft of this book, I was worried that no one would like it. So I kept it locked in my computer for 6 months, during which time I didn't even OPEN the Word document that contained it. I worried about sending it to literary agents and publishers because I was sure it would get rejected and that I wouldn't be strong enough to handle that critical feedback (*wrong!*).

Serendipity and the Start of the Success Snowball

I can say with absolute certainty that without encouragement from my family, friends, coaches, and blog readers (coupled with a few lucky signs from the universe), you would not be reading this book right now. My inner critics would have gotten the best of me because this is THE goal of my life—and, well, that is their favorite time to play.

With each step forward—writing the proposal, finding a literary agent, and pitching to publishers—I was risking rejection, but it felt great to finally take action. There were a few key moments and meetings that started creating a success snowball for me, and I held up my end of the bargain too—by pressing forward with my book project even though I could "fail" at any point.

Although I did get rejected by literary agents and publishers, there were a few who were interested and gave me very positive feedback, too. Getting the book deal with Running Press felt like clicking into my skis; I locked into my path and could finally see the finish line, no matter what moguls and rough spots I might encounter on the way there.

Unconditional Success

No matter how many books I sell, I feel successful knowing that I was able to realize my lifelong dream of being a published author, which is actually in service of a much larger and more important goal—to help others feel excited and happy about their lives. I hope—from the very bottom of my heart—that I have been able to help or inspire you in some way.

I can sleep at night knowing that I didn't give up on My Giant Life Goal; that I pushed through all the stuck, dark moments, listened to my gut, and found doorway after doorway that helped me move the project forward. By the time this book hits stores, it will have completed a 3-year trek through my brain, my computer, and my publishing company, and I am so grateful for everything I have learned along the way.

FINAL THOUGHTS

I am just like you. I am a human being, flawed and all. I am not perfect, and I do not have all the answers. I am fortunate to have a loving family, and I have had some very lucky breaks. But I have also worked hard, set goals, researched, networked, and struggled through big dips, ugly inner demons, and heartbreak and confusion, just like I am sure that you have too.

Though your formal education might be over, life after college is still about learning. Learning who you are, what you want, how to get it, and perhaps most important—how to relax and enjoy the ride. Be good to yourself; know that around the corner from every failure or disappointment there is a new opportunity waiting for you, and an army of people supporting you. Just let the inner-critic voices and dips serve as a sign that you are on exactly the right track!

I hope that through all of your ups and downs you continue to go after what you want, one day at a time. *Live big*! Life is too short to play small.

With big hugs and full of gratitude,

Jenny

APPENDIX:
The Essential Checklist

T HERE IS A LOT OF INFORMATION IN THIS BOOK. TO help you start taking action, below are essential next steps for each area of your life. In each section, there is a blank box for something that stood out to you as an action to take.

LIFE: YOUR BIG PICTURE

❏ Write your top 5 values on a Post-It. Stick it somewhere you can see it every day.

❏ Spend some time journaling about what you want each area of your life to look like.

❏ Make a list of three specific goals you want to accomplish in the next year. Choose one that's big and scary—but that would be thrilling to pursue.

❏ Add yours here:

_____

_____

WORK

- ❏ Take a few personality assessments (like Myers-Briggs or StrengthsFinder 2.0) to help identify potential career paths and articulate strengths to future employers. Collect results and store them in a "master file."
- ❏ Create a game plan for learning. What skills, knowledge, or experience will you need to land the job you want, or to make you invaluable in the one you have?
- ❏ Choose 3 people in careers or roles that interest you. Schedule them for lunch or coffee to learn about opportunities, build your network, and seek potential mentors.
- ❏ Add yours here:

MONEY

- ❏ Sign up for an online money management tool like Mint.com to track and manage your spending.
- ❏ Open an emergency savings account, separate from your everyday checking and savings accounts. Set up automatic monthly direct deposits to this account. Make sure you are also enrolled in your company's 401(k) plan if they have one.
- ❏ Set time aside to fully understand your current financial situation. In a given month, how much money is coming in? How much do you spend on essential expenses like rent and bills? How much is left over for discretionary spending?
- ❏ Add yours here:

HOME

- ❏ Buy a container of disposable cleaning wipes. Keep them under your kitchen and bathroom sinks for quick cleaning before guests come over.
- ❏ Put a donation box in your closet. Throw clothes in as you try them on if you know you will never wear them.
- ❏ Stock your medicine cabinet with the essentials: aspirin, Band-Aids, Neosporin, Tums, eye drops, calamine lotion, hydrogen peroxide, a gauze roll, and Sudafed and/or Claritin.
- ❏ Add yours here:

_____

_____

ORGANIZATION

- ❏ Create a spreadsheet for keeping phone numbers of service providers (health, car, etc.).
- ❏ Set up a calendar for tracking appointments, setting reminders, and staying on top of things.
- ❏ Buy a file box and set up folders for bills and important documents.
- ❏ Add yours here:

_____

_____

FRIENDS & FAMILY

- ❏ Schedule a reunion trip with your closest friends (far enough in advance so people can block the time off).
- ❏ Start a peer support group for a shared goal (fitness and nutrition) or topic of interest (leadership, time management).

- ❏ Make a list of ways to meet people in your area: volunteering, intramural sports, alumni groups, Toastmasters, networking clubs.
- ❏ Reflect on what you can do to improve your relationships with members of your family.
- ❏ Choose something actionable to focus on during your next interaction with them (or send your parents a thank-you note).
- ❏ Add yours here:

_____

_____

DATING & RELATIONSHIPS

- ❏ Make a list of your must-haves and deal-breakers in a future partner or relationship.
- ❏ Reflect on your areas of improvement (that if changed would have a positive impact on your current relationship and/or future partners).
- ❏ Make a list of lessons you've learned from previous relationships. What does it tell you about what you are looking for in the next one?
- ❏ Add yours here:

_____

_____

HEALTH

- ❏ Make a list of activities you enjoy. Schedule two fun outings in the next month.
- ❏ Identify your biggest struggle when it comes to food and exercise: what change would have the biggest impact?
- ❏ Hire a personal trainer or sign up for a fitness class if you can afford it (a one-time drop-in class counts!).

❏ Add yours here:

_____

_____

FUN & RELAXATION

❏ Make a list of 15 low-cost activities that make you happy.
❏ Identify 3 small things you can do each day to incorporate more fun and relaxation in your life.
❏ Create a life checklist of everything you want to do or try in your lifetime.
❏ Add yours here:

_____

_____

PERSONAL GROWTH

❏ Create your "why I'm great" file—a list of accomplishments, proudest moments, and qualities you can refer back to when times get tough and you need a confidence boost.
❏ Practice spending at least 5 minutes alone, in total silence, every day for the next week.
❏ Make a list of all the messages your inner critic sends over the next 2 weeks.
❏ Add yours here:

_____

_____

FINAL EXERCISE: NOTES TO SELF

Congratulations! You've come a long way. Hopefully the tips and exercises in this book have given you a lot to think about. Now you get to be the expert; after all, you know yourself better than I (or anyone else) ever could.

**What advice do you want to give yourself
as you embark on the next phase of your life?**

Acknowledgments

Mom: Thank you for helping me land so quickly on my feet after college. I have learned so much from you about life and work and independence, starting from the time I was a little girl. This book wouldn't be here without your many life lessons and practical tips. Thank you for all that you have done to help and support me through every transition—you are amazing. Oh—and I promise I will learn to cook one day!

Dad: Thank you for being an endless fount of insight and inspiration on our weekly walks; for being an eternal optimist, creator, and a dreamer. Thank you for keeping the dream of this book alive, and for reminding me that it would have helped people even in its earliest form two years ago. I've sent 10,000 good luck karma points your way as a thank-you for all of the priceless copy edits and suggestions.

To my brother Tom: T-Bones you are an absolute genius and the best supporter I could ever ask for. Your tenacity, drive, passion, confidence, enthusiasm, encouragement, and unbelievable sense of humor have me convinced that I am THE luckiest sister on the planet. Oh—and I'm sorry for making you play school by filling out fake worksheets when we were kids. I like to think you learned something? Who knew I would be turning exercises just like those into a book one day.

To my grandparents: Thank you for always believing in me. Grandma—you called this book on the day I was born when you said, "Jenny Blake—that sounds like an author's name. She is going to be published someday." You were right! Thank you both for helping me reach my biggest "life after college" milestones; your support and encouragement mean so much to me.

To Sarah Lazin, my literary agent and Jennifer Kasius, my editor: This book simply would not be here without you. Thank you for seeing the potential in me and this project, and for helping it forward at every stage. It is absolutely an honor to be working with both of you. Thanks also to Susan Blair at National Geographic, whose interest and encouragement gave me the confidence to pick this project back up after months of writer's block. **Mark Hanaeur:** Thank you for the fabulous headshots (26 years after my first photo shoot with you). **Bob Gordon:** Thank you for the sage legal advice and for introducing me to Sarah! Big thanks also to David and Regan Harrington.

Many thanks to the other great folks at Running Press who contributed to the project: Susan Hom for your fantastic copy-edits; Amanda Richmond for doing such a brilliant job with layout and design; Craig Herman for your help with marketing and promotion, and any other behind-the-scenes contributors I might have missed.

To the coaches who have changed my life: Ruth Ann Harnisch, Erik Mazziota, Jenny Ferry, Barbara Fittipaldi, Jeff Jacobson, Steve Maxwell, and Adrian Klaphaak. Thank you for helping me see my dreams, for holding my highest vision even when I couldn't see it myself, and for encouraging me at every turn. Words simply cannot express my gratitude for all of you. **Ruth Ann:** Thank you for your brilliant coaching, and for helping me break through my upper limits. Your countless (and priceless) life lessons and wise words will stay with me forever.

To my book (and life) mentors: Susan Biali, Chris Guillebeau (the founding member of the Jenny Blake Advisory Board), Michael Larsen, Phil Villarreal, and Kevin Smokler. Thank you all for believing in me as an author even when you'd only just met me, and for sharing your mistakes and missteps in the hopes that I wouldn't make the same ones. Thank you for always being available for questions no matter how busy you were, and for your endless encouragement and support. You are amazing role models, and I'm lucky to have you in my life!

To Lynn Vavreck and Doug Rivers: Thank you for taking a chance on me when I was 20 years old. Working at Polimetrix was truly a once-in-a-lifetime opportunity—I learned SO much from both of you and from the many company hats I was fortunate enough to wear. **Leen:** I still don't know how to cook a sweet potato, but I'd be happy to adjudicate a race for you any time.

To my angels: Julie Clow, Tara Canobbio, Elisa Doucette, Jenny Ferry, and Jeremy Orr—You have lifted me up through countless roller coasters, empty spaces, success demons, inner critics, dips, and depressions throughout the course of this book project. But most of all? You helped me celebrate when it barely felt real. When I was still in shock that this was actually happening, you were right there giving me hugs, taking me out for lemon drop martinis, squealing with glee, and baking two-dozen cupcakes with Snickers and cookie dough in the middle. Thank you for being the best friends a girl could ask for.

Julie Clow: Thank you for your countless edits, laser sharp strategy sessions, brainstorming, and sanity checks throughout this project. I am so lucky to have a friend as brilliant as you are; and one with whom I can share not just book ideas, but yoga, workouts, dinners, work nights in and fun nights out. You are incredible.

Jenny Ferry: You have been by my side every step of the way. You have been a bright, shining light throughout this project (and in my life).

Big hugs also to the special friends who directly shaped and encouraged me throughout this project: Gil Knox, Sharalyn Hartwell, Maddy Dray, Megan Deino, Jamie Varon, Margaret Coblentz, Laura Ottersen, Emily Schuman, Amy Irlanda, Erin McGranahan, Megan Stichter, Vanessa Mayle, Lauren Jew, Laura Boyd, Kristi Richey, Benjy Feen, Jun Loayza, Andrea Owen, Stacy Kruse, Katya Kingston, Chelsea Latimer, Eve Ellenbogen, Andrew Weitsman, Ann Elizabeth Grace, Nate St. Pierre, J-Money, Ryan Knapp, Jay Schryer, ChaChanna Simpson, Willie Jackson, Grace Boyle, Ryan Stephens, Derek Shanahan, Ryan Paugh, Doniree Walker, Molly Hoyne Mahar, Srinivas Rao, Dani, Paul Williams, Katie Czerepak, Greg Blencoe, Joy Agcongay, Barbara Demarest, Mike Robbins, Becky Cotton, Lori Hodgson, Tina Lifford, Pamela Slim, Lindsey Pollak, Ben Casnocha, Shannon Cooney, DS, and my NYC Angel, Ann Turi.

To my teachers—Marianne Chowning, Kim Acker, Susan Fox and Lynn Vavreck: You may have thought you were teaching me about math, yoga, and political science, but you have also taught me about what it means to show up as a fabulous woman in this world. Thank you for inspiring me to be driven, funny, friendly, successful, well-rounded, down-to-earth, and generally just a kick-ass woman.

To the inside scoop book subscribers: you made this project so much fun! Thank you for following and supporting me at every stage of this process. Knowing that you were there and being able to share with you at every turn meant so much.

To the book respondents and contributors: A huge thank you to all of you who replied on Twitter and to the survey. Your contributions to this book were invaluable. **Special thanks to the #u30pro crew:** Lauren Fernandez, Scott Hale, and David Spinks, who helped me launch a world-class Twitter campaign at the last minute.

To my blog readers and all of the fellow twenty-something bloggers I "grew up" with: Thank you from the bottom of my heart. I would not be here without you. You have propped me up, kept me going, given me encouragement, and have made me infinitely smarter with every comment and every e-mail. I cherish you. You have truly changed *my* life. Thank you.

To my book readers (that's you!): I feel incredibly honored and privileged to share this book and my ideas with you. Thank you so much for spending your valuable time and attention with me.

To anyone and everyone I forgot—I'm sorry and I love you!

About Jenny Blake

JENNY STARTED WORKING AT GOOGLE IN 2006, WHERE she currently serves as a career development program manager and internal coach. Her role involves coaching, manager training, and building scalable solutions to help Googlers focus on their personal growth and career development.

While working at Google, Jenny completed training to be a life coach through the Coaches Training Institute in 2008, and finished her certification in 2010. She is a certified Myers-Briggs practitioner, and served on the Board of Governors for the International Association of Coaching in 2010. Jenny also completed yoga teacher training in 2010 through the White Lotus Foundation in Santa Barbara.

Prior to Google and halfway through her junior year at UCLA, Jenny took a leave of absence to help launch a political polling start-up company, Polimetrix (later acquired and renamed YouGov America), with her college professor and mentor. For two years she served as the office manager, marketing assistant, and webmaster.

Jenny returned to finish at UCLA in the spring of 2005. She graduated in 3 years with degrees in political science and communications, and with several distinctions: Phi Beta Kappa, Magna Cum Laude, and College Honors.

About the Blog

After stumbling through the "real world" largely on her own, Jenny felt compelled to share her knowledge with other young professionals. The experience of leaving school before her friends and her love of teaching others inspired her to launch LifeAfterCollege.org in 2005.

Jenny's goal is to help people focus on the BIG picture of their lives ... not just the details. She does this through her blog by providing simple, practical tips about life, work, money, happiness, personal growth and more.

Just for Fun

Jenny LOVES cupcakes, coffee, and personal development books. Dogs, dancing, gadgets, yoga, watching football, writing, Moleskine notebooks, and travel make her pretty happy too.

Jenny is also obsessed with personality tests—in fact here is everything you will ever need to know about her: she is a Myers-Briggs ENFJ, an Enneagram Type 3 Achiever, a Keirsey Idealist/Teacher and a True Colors blue/orange. Her StrengthsFinder strengths are: Relator, Strategic, Learner, Achiever, and Activator.

Follow Jenny on Twitter @jenny_blake, or visit LifeAfterCollege.org to download templates, subscribe to blog updates, or to learn more about her coaching, training, and speaking services.

Have thoughts on the book? Suggestions, struggles, or success stories to share?

I would love to hear from you! Please feel free to e-mail me at jenny@lifeaftercollege.org.

Want to help spread the word?

If you enjoyed the book and think others could benefit, I would be forever grateful if you could help in any of the following ways:

- Leave a review on Amazon.com to help others decide whether to purchase a copy
- Buy a copy for a friend or relative as a gift
- Let your networks know if you found the book helpful by posting on Facebook or sending a tweet with the hashtag #LACBook to share your thoughts
- Join the Life After College community at Facebook.com/LifeAfterCollege
- Subscribe to blog updates at LifeAfterCollege.org
- Visit the book's website for additional resources: LACbook.com

Your word-of-mouth support is much appreciated!

As one of my book mentors, Michael Larsen, says, "Authors and publishers don't keep books alive; readers do."

Thank you for helping me keep this book (and dream) alive.

Notes

Notes

Notes

Notes

Notes

Notes

Notes

Notes

Notes

Notes